Trends in
Organizational Behavior

Volume 6
THE VIRTUAL ORGANIZATION

Trends in Organizational Behavior

Volume 6
THE VIRTUAL ORGANIZATION

Edited by

Cary L. Cooper

Manchester School of Management, University of Manchester Institute of
Science and Technology, UK

and

Denise M. Rousseau

Carnegie Mellon University, Pittsburgh, USA

JOHN WILEY & SONS, LTD

Chichester · New York · Weinheim · Brisbane · Singapore · Toronto

Trends in Organizational Behavior, Volume 6

Published as a supplement to the *Journal of Organizational Behavior, Volume 20*

Other Wiley Editorial Offices

John Wiley & Sons, Inc., 605 Third Avenue,
New York, NY 10158-0012, USA

Wiley-VCH Verlag GmbH, Pappelallee 3,
D-69469 Weinheim, Germany

Jacaranda Wiley Ltd, 33 Park Road, Milton,
Queensland 4064, Australia

John Wiley & Sons (Asia) Pte Ltd, 2 Clementi Loop #02-01,
Jin Xing Distripark, Singapore 129809

John Wiley & Sons (Canada) Ltd, 22 Worcester Road,
Rexdale, Ontario M9W 1L1, Canada

British Library Cataloguing in Publication Data

A catalogue record for this book is available from the British Library

ISBN 0-471-89943-7

Typeset in 10/12 pt Palatino by Dorwyn Ltd, Rowlands Castle, Hants.
Printed and bound in Great Britain by Bookcraft (Bath) Ltd, Midsomer Norton.
This book is printed on acid-free paper responsibly manufactured from sustainable
forestry, in which at least two trees are planted for each one used in paper production.

Contents

About the Editors

CARY L. COOPER

Currently BUPA Professor of Organizational Psychology and Health at the Manchester School of Management (UMIST) and Pro-Vice-Chancellor of the University of Manchester Institute of Science and Technology. Professor Cooper is the author of over 80 books (on stress, women at work, and industrial and organizational psychology), has written over 250 articles for academic journals, and is a frequent contributor to national newspapers, TV and radio. He is President of the British Academy of Management, Founding Editor of the *Journal of Organizational Behavior*, and a Fellow of the British Psychological Society, the Royal Society of Arts, the Royal Society of Medicine, Royal Society of Health, the Academy of Management and the British Academy of Management. He is also Co-Editor, with Chris Argyris, of the twelve-volume *Encyclopedia of Management* (Blackwell); and Co-Editor of *Stress Medicine* and the *International Journal of Management Reviews*.

DENISE M. ROUSSEAU

Denise Rousseau H. J. Heinz II Professor of Organizational Behavior and Public Policy at Carnegie Mellon University, jointly in the Heinz School of Public Policy and Management and in the Graduate School of Industrial Administration. She has been a faculty member at Northwestern University, the University of Michigan, and the Naval Postgraduate School.

Her research addresses the impact of work group processes on performance and the changing psychological contract at work. Rousseau is an author of more than 80 articles which have appeared in prominent academic journals, such as the *Journal of Applied Psychology, Academy of Management Review*, and *Administrative Science Quarterly*. She is currently Editor-in-Chief of the *Journal of Organizational Behavior*. Her other books include: *Psychological Contracts in Organizations: Understanding Written and*

Unwritten Agreements (Sage); the *Trends in Organizational Behavior* series (Wiley) with Cary Cooper, *Developing an Interdisciplinary Science of Organizations* (Jossey-Bass) with Karlene Roberts and Charles Hulin; *The Boundaryless Career* (Oxford) with Michael Arthur; *Psychological Contracts in Employment: Cross-National Perspectives* (Sage, in press) with Rene Schalk; and *Relational Wealth* (Oxford, in press) with Carrie Leana.

Professor Rousseau has consulted in diverse organizations and written numerous articles for managers and executives including "Teamwork: inside and out" (*Business Week/Advance*), "Managing diversity for high performance" (*Business Week/Advance*) and "Two ways to change (and keep) the psychological contract" (*Academy of Management Executive*). She has taught in executive programs at Northwestern (Kellogg), Cornell, Carnegie Mellon and in industry programs for health care, journalism and manufacturing among others.

She is a Fellow in the American Psychological Association, Society for Industrial and Organizational Psychology, and the Academy of Management.

List of Contributors

Wayne F. Cascio	Graduate School of Business, University of Colorado, Denver, USA
Susan G. Cohen	Marshall School of Business, University of Southern California, USA
Kevin Daniels	Sheffield University Management School, University of Sheffield, UK
Gerardine DeSanctis	Fuqua School of Business, Duke University, USA
Raghu Garud	New York University, USA
Jessica Lipnack	NetAge Inc., Massachusetts, USA
Don Mankin	Marshall School of Business, University of Southern California, USA
Susan Albers Mohrman	Marshall School of Business, University of Southern California, USA
Sumita Raghuram	Fordham University, USA
Charles C. Snow	The Smeal College of Business Administration, The Pennsylvania State University, USA
Paul R. Sparrow	Sheffield University Management School, University of Sheffield, UK
Jeffrey Stamps	NetAge Inc., Massachusetts, USA
Nancy Staudenmayer	Fuqua School of Business, Duke University, USA
Batia M. Wiesenfeld	New York University, USA
Sze Sze Wong	Fuqua School of Business, Duke University, USA

Editorial Introduction

The *Trends in Organizational Behavior* series has been the vehicle by which new concepts and innovative ideas could be explored in subject areas where little systematic organizational behavior research has been conducted. It was conceptualized as a TV magazine program, with up-to-date issues highlighted in a short, hopefully incisive, way and published swiftly—a kind of straight "off the press" organizational behavior research item. In the past, we have put together a wide range of topics in one volume, but in this volume we decided to concentrate on a single theme, but from different perspectives. The theme here is Virtual Organizations. As more and more people become contingent or short term contract workers, and as new technology makes remote working increasingly possible, the problems, opportunities and challenges of working in virtual organizations is an absolute reality of the first decade of the next millennium.

The chapters included in this volume provide fertile ground for framing the research agenda in an important area of organizational behavior left virtually untouched. We explore here the implications of virtual workplaces, the promises/payoffs and potentially negative or self-threats of virtual organizations, the human resource management implications and associated future research issues, the context of geography and networks, and the interdependencies involved in creating and maintaining such organizations. In terms of collaboration in virtual organizations, we also explore the areas of conflict resolution, process facilitation and team design, the psychology of flow and optimal expertise and computer-supported cooperative work.

We hope this volume will encourage our readers to create more innovative research designs in exploring the virtual organizations of the future.

CLC
DMR

CHAPTER 1

Virtual Workplaces: Implications for Organizational Behavior

Wayne F. Cascio
Graduate School of Business, University of Colorado, Denver, USA

INTRODUCTION

Consider the new paradigm of work—anytime, anywhere, in real space or in cyberspace. For many employers the virtual workplace, in which employees operate remotely from each other and from managers, is a reality now, and all indications are that it will become even more prevalent in the future. In and of itself, this represents a dramatic change in how we work, and it presents new challenges for employees, managers, and students of organizational behavior. The challenges stem from the physical separation of workers and managers wrought by such information-age arrangements as teleworking virtual teams. "How can I manage them if I can't see them?" is a question that many managers are now asking. This simple question has far-ranging implications for individual behavior and organizational structures. The most fundamental of these implications involves attitudes and beliefs.

Many such attitudes and beliefs are founded in an approach to designing work and organizations that is rapidly becoming obsolete. At its core is the concept of *functional specialization*—slotting workers into narrowly-defined jobs. Both the economist Adam Smith (1776) and the engineer Charles Babbage (1832) described some of the benefits of such specialization: uniform-quality production, faster production, and a higher level of worker skill in the narrow area of specialization.

Trends in Organizational Behavior, Volume 6. Edited by C. L. Cooper and D. M. Rousseau.
Copyright © 1999 John Wiley & Sons, Ltd.

Although the basic concepts of functional specialization were well-developed by the late 18th century, it was not until the late 19th and early 20th centuries that a systematic scheme for designing work was developed and widely popularized by Frederick W. Taylor. It was embodied in the approach known as "Scientific Management". These ideas focused on the systematic analysis and breakdown of work into its smallest mechanical elements, and then their rearrangement into the most efficient combination (Bell, 1972). Taylor's goal was to obtain more production from workers at less cost to management, thereby permitting higher rates of pay for the workers. Indeed, he was trying to institute a kind of social physics. Once the work was scientifically mapped out, he felt, there could be no disputes about how hard one should work or the pay one should receive for his or her labor (Bell, 1972). These principles have strongly influenced industrial society's approach to job design, even to the present day.

Yet at least two of the basic principles seem less applicable in the Information Age. First, narrow functional specialists are being replaced by cross-trained, multi-functional specialists. The reason for this is that firms need to respond more rapidly than ever before to changes in the marketplace, and downsizing and reengineering have left many organizations with fewer workers. Those that remain have to be multi-skilled, and if they are multi-skilled in more than one functional area, they are especially valuable to their organizations. Cross-functional teams will benefit from such multi-skilling, because they should be able to share information rapidly, to assimilate that information in a manner that will facilitate quick decisions, and to learn as a group to improve their own ability to function. However, suppose these teams are virtual in nature, and do not actually meet face-to-face? There is almost no empirical information on whether the same kinds of benefits will ensue.

A second principle that seems less applicable in the Information Age is that of rigid separation of managing and supervising from working. Consider self-managing work groups as an example. Such groups are defined by three characteristics (Hackman, 1990):

(1) They are real, meaning that they are intact, identifiable social systems, even if they are small or temporary.
(2) They are work groups that have to do a specified piece of work that results in a product, service, or decision whose acceptability is measurable.
(3) They are self-managing groups whose members have the authority to manage their own task and interpersonal processes as they carry out their work.

Such groups are part of a broader sociotechnical system. A rigorous, three-year evaluation of self-managing work groups in a non-union British company that produces confectionery products for home and export markets found that the self-managing group design produced a strong and sustained effect on employees' satisfaction with the work itself, and a more temporary effect on their satisfaction with the work environment, including pay, but it had no effect on work motivation or job performance. The approach also produced clear economic benefits. With responsibility for decision making delegated to the shop floor, the need for supervision declined, indirect labor costs decreased, and productivity benefits increased (Wall et al., 1986).

Can an individual serve as a member of a self-managing work group if he or she is not physically present along with other members of the group? In theory, the answer is yes, but as we shall see, there are some potential obstacles to effective team performance under these circumstances. It is technology that makes virtual workplaces possible (Cascio, 1998), and in the following section we will examine how and why this is so.

TECHNOLOGY: ENABLER OF THE VIRTUAL WORKPLACE

Without information and knowledge, workers in virtual workplaces become emasculated and ineffective. Fortunately technology and enlightened management practices can ensure that this does not happen. Where we work, when we work, and how we communicate are being revolutionized, as a "seamless" web of electronic communications media—e-mail, voice mail, cellular telephones, laptops with modems, hand-held organizers, video conferencing, and interactive pagers—make teamwork and mobility a reality. Not only is work becoming seamless as it moves between home, office, and phone, but it also is becoming endless as it rolls through a 24-hour day (Power Gizmos, 1997). Consider some of the business reasons that are driving the trend toward virtual workplaces.

- **Reduced real estate expenses**—IBM saves 40 to 60 per cent per site annually by eliminating offices for all employees except those that truly need them.
- **Increased productivity**—internal IBM studies show gains of 15 to 40 per cent. US West reported that the productivity of its telecommuting employees increased, some by as much as 40 per cent (Matthes, 1992).
- **High profits**—Hewlett-Packard doubled revenue per salesperson after moving its sales people to virtual workplace arrangements (O'Connell, 1996).

• **Improved customer service**—Andersen Consulting found that its consultants spent 25 per cent more "face time" with customers when they did not have permanent offices (O'Connell, 1996).

Of course all of these gains are not free. The additional cost required to equip a mobile or home worker varies from roughly US$3,000 to $5,000, plus about $1,000 in upgrades and supplies every year thereafter (Clark, 1997). In addition, to be viable, virtual offices require four types of information:

(1) Online materials that can be downloaded and printed
(2) Databases on products and customers that are accessible from remote locations
(3) Well-indexed, automated central files that are accessible from remote locations
(4) A way to track the location of mobile workers

WHEN VIRTUAL WORK ARRANGEMENTS ARE APPROPRIATE

Virtual workplaces are not appropriate for all jobs. Jobs in sales, marketing, and consulting seem to be suited best, although even in these jobs, virtual work arrangements are not recommended for new employees or those who are new to a position. The key is to work with employees well ahead of planned transitions. Firms such as Lotus, IBM, and Hewlett-Packard have written guidelines, training, and networks of peers to facilitate the transition. For example, Hewlett-Packard's guidelines for virtual workplaces address topics such as who can participate, family and household issues, remote office setup, and administrative processes. Here is a profile of the successful remote employee. He or she is:

• Familiar and comfortable with the job (not newly-hired or promoted)
• Self-motivated; does not need high structure and detailed instructions in order to work effectively
• An effective communicator, both orally and in writing
• Adaptable, able to compromise
• Knowledgeable about organizational procedures
• Technically self-sufficient
• Results-oriented

Just as not all employees are suited to work away from their primary business locations during scheduled work hours, not all managers are suited to manage employees with virtual work arrangements. Those who are seem to have the following characteristics:

- High trust in employees to perform their duties while away from direct supervision
- An open, positive attitude that focuses on solutions to issues rather than on seeking excuses to discontinue virtual work arrangements
- A results-oriented management style that emphasizes outcomes, not processes
- Effective communicator, whether formally or informally, and whether employees are working remotely or at the primary business location
- Able to delegate effectively, and to follow up to ensure that work is accomplished

Can formal screening programs be developed to identify in advance individuals who might be suited well to work and manage in a virtual environment? Work-samples that engage individuals and simulate remote operations seem most appropriate, for they will provide the most realistic previews of the new work arrangements. Video-based realistic previews that illustrate concisely a "Day in the Life of" a member of a virtual team or e-telecommuter, may be especially helpful. Subsequently the screening programs should be validated in order to assess whether or not they really are capable of classifying individuals properly as suited or not suited to work under virtual conditions.

Assuming that virtual work arrangements are appropriate, and that employees with the "right" profile are available, how should a manager proceed? Two types of virtual work arrangements that are becoming more popular are virtual teams and teleworking. Let's consider each of these briefly.

Virtual Teams

In a virtual team, members' primary interaction is through some combination of electronic communication systems. Members may never "meet" in the traditional sense (Clark, 1997). Such an arrangement provides several advantages:

(1) It saves time, travel expenses, and eliminates lack of access to experts
(2) Teams can be organized whether or not members are in reasonable proximity to each other
(3) Firms can use outside consultants without incurring expenses for travel, lodging, and downtime
(4) Virtual teams allow firms to expand their potential labor markets, enabling them to hire and retain the best people regardless of their physical location
(5) Employees can accommodate both personal and professional lives

(6) Dynamic team membership allows people to move from one project to another
(7) Employees can be assigned to multiple, concurrent teams
(8) Team communications and work reports are available online to facilitate swift responses to the demands of a global market. For example, Veriphone uses a "relay race" to develop software products faster than its competitors. Here is how it works. Software engineers at Dallas headquarters work a full day on a project, then put their work product online on the company's intranet. As the Dallas employees are leaving work, their Veriphone counterparts in Honolulu are arriving. The Honolulu engineers begin working where their Dallas counterparts left off. They then work a full day, and hand over their work product to their Veriphone counterparts in Bombay, who are just coming to work. As the Bombay software engineers are leaving work, they transmit their work product electronically back to headquarters in Dallas, where their counterparts are just arriving for the next day's work. Electronic communications media make the relay race possible. Clients benefit from the firm's speedy response to their needs.

Of course the major disadvantages of virtual teams are the lack of physical interaction—with its associated verbal and non-verbal cues—and the synergies that often accompany face-to-face communication. In high-context cultures, such as those in the Middle East and Asia, what is not said is often more important than what is said. Can workers in those cultures adapt to a virtual team arrangement? There is little or no research evidence to go on, but it is an engaging hypothesis that workers in low-context cultures, such as English-speaking countries where it is possible to be very precise with words, will report higher levels of satisfaction and productivity when working in virtual teams than their counterparts in high-context cultures.

Despite these drawbacks, virtual teams are growing in popularity. "Groupware", computer-based systems explicitly designed to support groups of people working together, enables virtual interactions (Ishii, Kobayashi & Arita, 1994). The goal of groupware technology, from e-mail to company-based intranets, is simple: to promote and improve interaction among individuals (Aannestad & Hooper, 1997). This is collaborative empowerment.

Training Members and Managers of Virtual Teams

A 1996 survey conducted by Dale Carnegie Training found that 90 per cent of American workers spend at least part of their work day in a team situation, yet only about half received any formal teamwork training. Virtual teams add another layer of complexity to any teamwork situation. They have created a rich training agenda, for example:

- How to use the software to enhance team performance
- How to manage the anonymous environment, and when to use it
- How to provide anonymous participation and feedback when ideas or criticism need to be brought out. This is particularly important since the traditional cues of social interaction—body language and hand gestures—may not be available
- Social protocol for virtual teams—for example, how to express displeasure or anger; how to criticize processes or performance without assigning blame to any single individual; how to express praise
- Since changes in team membership must occur with seamless continuity, it is important to teach common culture values—for example, team membership may change frequently, and it is not personal

Implications of Virtual Teams for Organizational Behavior

Perhaps the most common forms of virtual teams are task forces and project teams. These are temporary groups (e.g., in legal cases, consulting projects, or within-company task forces). Such teams are formed specifically to solve a particular problem or to perform a specific task. When the problem has been solved or the task completed, the virtual team disappears and team members go back to their normal duties. As Gersick and Davis-Sacks (1990) have noted, task forces and project teams have an unusual mix of autonomy and dependence. On one hand, they typically are free, within broad limits, to proceed with the work in whatever way members find appropriate. On the other hand, they do their work at the behest of some other person or group, and therefore members depend considerably on their client's preferences.

In a virtual team, patterns of authority and social interaction are very different from those of a team that interacts physically, such as an operating-room team or a basketball team. To function as a team, it is necessary to have some real interdependencies among team members. Otherwise all that remains is a loosely-coupled group. It is important, therefore, to define roles clearly so that members can collaborate to accomplish work. It is also important to have a clear leadership structure in order to minimize ambiguity about who has the right to decide what (Hackman, 1990). Ground rules like these are even more imperative in a virtual team, because of the physical separation of members from clients and each other.

Teleworking

Another form of virtual work arrangement is teleworking (also known as telecommuting); that is, work carried out in a location that is remote from central offices or production facilities, where the worker has no personal contact with co-workers, but is able to communicate with them using electronic means (Gupta, Karimi & Somers, 1995). As of late 1997, roughly 11 million U.S. workers teleworked, a 30 per cent increase since 1995, according to a study by AT&T (Jackson, 1997). Two of every three *Fortune 500* companies now employ teleworkers. In addition to work-at-home arrangements, teleworking may assume at least three other forms:

- *Hoteling*—At Ernst & Young in Washington, D.C., workers call a central reservations center, provide a personal identification code, along with the date that space is needed. Available space includes workstations and meeting rooms. On arrival, the employee's name is on an office door, and requested files and supplies are inside. Phone numbers are forwarded, and a concierge is available. Ernst & Young has hoteled eight offices and is converting seven more. It has found that the longer workers hotel, the less they focus on the office and more on the customer ("The new workplace", 1996).
- *"Hot desking"*—20,000 IBM employees, primarily those in sales and service, share offices with four people, on average. Cisco Systems, a technology firm in San Jose, CA, has several thousand people sharing a variety of spaces around the world. As we noted earlier, however, hoteling and hot desking are not for everyone ("Office hoteling", 1997).
- *Telework centers*—These are corporate office environments in miniature that offer more technology than an employee has at home. Located in residential neighborhoods, small groups of employees report to work near home, rather than commute. Centers, such as the Ontario Telebusiness Work Center in Southern California, offer electronically-equipped suites to companies (O'Connell, 1996). The advantage: a suburban location minimizes commuting time, while maximizing productive time.

Effect of Teleworking on Productivity and Adjustment

When teleworking is appropriate in a given situation (right job, right person, right reason, right boss) firms report that people's strategic planning skills go up dramatically because they have blocks of time to think (Warner, 1997). People themselves say they are as much as 40 per cent more productive while working away from the office, because they have fewer distractions. While such self-report data are encouraging, they do not substitute for rigorous empirical research on this issue. There is a pressing need for empirical research to inform decision makers, as the numbers of organizations and individuals that adopt such arrangements increase year by year in developed countries everywhere.

It is also important to note that if people are coerced into work-at-home arrangements, they may rebel or fail to develop the kinds of work habits that will enable them to be productive. Can parents with pre-school-age children work at home in a productive manner? Can workers who have been supervised closely in their jobs for years adapt to the near-total autonomy that teleworking provides? Can they learn to focus on results rather than simply efforts (e.g., "being seen" at the office working either early or late?)

Finally, it is important to address the political implications of teleworking arrangements. "Out of sight, out of mind" is still very true in many organizations. Might teleworkers be unwittingly sacrificing access to desirable assignments or career-enhancing positions because they and their work are not noticed by key gatekeepers in an organization? How might organizational structures be modified to ensure that teleworkers are afforded the same considerations as their office-based counterparts? These are pressing questions for which we as a profession do not yet have answers.

Some possible remedies include the following. Teleworkers need to send a few more voice mails and e-mails to keep the boss informed, and technology makes this possible—laptops and computer servers that give mobile employees access to company files. "Mix and match" arrangements, in which workers spend one or two days a week at the office, where they can interact with managers and co-workers, seem to work best. In fact, AT&T found in its 1997 survey, that one third of teleworkers would look for other work if they were forced back into the office fold! More than 70 per cent reported that they were more satisfied with their jobs than before they started teleworking, and 75 per cent reported feeling more satisfied with their personal and family lives than before starting work at home, for reasons including better relations with spouses and children, improved morale, and less stress (Jackson, 1997).

Virtual Office Challenges for Managers

By far the biggest challenge is performance management ("If I can't see employees, how do I know that they are working?"). This is not the same thing as performance appraisal, an exercise that many managers do once a year to identify and discuss job-relevant strengths and weaknesses of individuals or teams. In contrast, performance management is part of a continuous process of improvement over time. It demands daily, not annual, attention.

At a general level, the broad process of performance management requires that managers do three things well: define performance, facilitate performance, and encourage performance (Cascio, 1996). These principles certainly apply to conventional working arrangements, but they are even more important in virtual work arrangements, because of the physical separation of workers and managers from each other. Let's consider each of these.

Define performance—individual employees or teams must know what is expected of them. As an example, consider a self-managed work team, where members will be physically separated from each other. To be successful, a fundamental requirement is that each team member understand his or her responsibilities. A manager trying to define performance might ask the following questions of the members of the team to help clarify these responsibilities:

Do you expect each team member to fulfill more than one role on the team?

Do you expect team members to learn each other's jobs?

Which responsibilities will team members share (e.g., selecting new members, rating each other's performance)?

Exactly how will team members share these responsibilities?

Will the team elect a leader? What responsibilities will this person have?

Who is responsible for disciplinary action, if the need arises?

How will the team make decisions (e.g., by consensus, majority rule)?

Which decisions does the team have the authority to make?

The next step is to develop specific, challenging goals, measures of the extent to which goals have been accomplished, and assessment mechanisms so that workers and managers can stay focused on what really counts. Goals such as "make the company successful" are too vague to be useful. In a productive partnership, managers and employees should jointly agree on performance measures, such as the volume of advertising revenue generated per quarter by an account executive of a cable television company, or the average time taken to respond to a customer's inquiry. As we noted earlier, this is no different, in principle, from the kinds of joint decisions that are made in conventional working environments.

To be useful, the measures should be linked to the strategic direction, business objectives, and customer requirements for the company

(Moravec, 1996). For a cable television company, a major strategic thrust might be to increase the number of new subscribers, or the number of current subscribers who pay for premium channels. For a firm that provides outsourcing services in information technology, major customer requirements might be timeliness of response to inquiries, and cost savings relative to in-house capability.

In defining performance, the third requirement is assessment. This is where performance appraisal comes in. Regular assessment of progress toward goals focuses the attention and efforts of an employee or team. A manager who takes the time to identify measurable goals, but then fails to assess progress towards them, is asking for trouble. "Mix-and-match" work arrangements lend themselves nicely to periodic meetings of workers and managers where the agenda is to assess progress toward goals.

The overall objective of goals, measures, and assessment is to leave no doubt about what is expected of individuals, and, if appropriate, teams, how it will be measured, and where individuals or teams stand at any given point in time. These kinds of "ground rules" are important in conventional organizational structures, but they are essential in virtual work environments, because of the physical separation of team members and managers from each other. There should be no surprises in the performance management process—and regular feedback to remote employees helps ensure that there won't be.

Facilitate performance. Managers who are committed to managing for maximum performance recognize that one of their major responsibilities is to eliminate roadblocks to successful performance. Another is to provide adequate resources to get a job done right and on time, and a third is to pay careful attention to selecting employees.

What are some examples of **obstacles** that can inhibit maximum performance in a virtual work environment? Consider just a few: delays in receiving critical information, inability to access centrally-maintained files and databases from remote locations, and inefficient design of work processes. Employees are well aware of these, and they are only too willing to identify them—if managers will just ask for their input. Then it is the manager's job to eliminate these obstacles.

Having eliminated roadblocks to successful performance, the next step is to **provide adequate resources**—capital resources, material resources, or human resources. After all, if remote employees lack the tools to reach the challenging goals they have set, they will become frustrated and disenchanted. Indeed, one observer has gone so far as to say "It's immoral not to give people tools to meet tough goals (Kerr, 1995)". Conversely, employees really appreciate it when their employer provides everything they need to perform well. Not surprisingly, they usually do perform well under those circumstances.

A final aspect of performance facilitation is the **careful selection of employees**. After all, the last thing any manager wants is to have people who are ill-suited to their jobs (or virtual work arrangements) by temperament or training, because this often leads to overstaffing, excessive labor costs, and reduced productivity. As we noted earlier, work samples and realistic job previews of remote working arrangements can be extremely helpful in avoiding costly selection errors. Managers who are truly committed to managing for maximum performance pay attention to all of the details—all of the factors that might affect performance—and leave nothing to chance.

In a virtual environment, this requires a break with the tradition of everyday supervision and contact with employees. Rather, for employees it implies greater self-management, more autonomy, and lots of opportunities to experiment, take risks, and be entrepreneurial. The manager's job is to define performance, to eliminate obstacles that inhibit maximum performance, and to provide adequate resources for employees to accomplish their work. In a virtual work environment, these tasks require a variety of modes of planned communication—from e-mail to voice mail, to video conferencing, and, perhaps most importantly, periodic face-to-face communication.

Encourage performance. This is the last area of management responsibility in a coordinated approach to performance management. To encourage performance, especially repeated good performance, it is important to do three more things well: (**1**) provide a sufficient amount of rewards that employees really value, (**2**) in a timely, (**3**) fair manner.

Don't bother to offer rewards that nobody cares about, like a gift certificate to see a fortune teller. On the contrary, it makes sense to begin by asking employees at all levels what is most important to them—for example, pay, benefits, free time, merchandise, or opportunities for professional development. Then consider tailoring the organizational awards program so that employees or teams can choose from a menu of similarly-valued options.

Next, **provide rewards in a timely manner**, soon after major accomplishments. For example, a metal-stamping plant in San Leandro, California, North American Tool & Die, provides monthly cash awards for creativity. This is important, for if there is an excessive delay between effective performance and receipt of the reward, then the reward loses its potential to motivate subsequent high performance. In a virtual work environment, timely rewards are even more important in order to avoid the perception that remote employees are "out of sight, out of mind".

Finally, provide rewards in a manner that employees consider **fair**. Fairness is a subjective concept, and it depends on a comparison between the rewards a person receives for his or her contributions to the organization, and some comparison standard. Such a standard might be:

- Others—a comparison with what similarly-situated others received, either inside or outside the organization
- Self—a comparison with a person's own rewards and contributions at a different time or with that same person's evolving views of what he or she is worth
- Systems—a comparison with what the organization has promised

Not surprisingly, employees often behave very responsibly when they are asked in advance for their opinions about what is fair. Indeed, it only seems fair to ask them!

In summary, managing for maximum performance requires that managers do three things well: define performance, facilitate performance, and encourage performance. Like a compass, the role of the manager is to provide orientation, direction, and feedback.

In managing a virtual workplace a second major challenge is communication. It is important not to over-rely on e-mail, which is one-way communication. In addition to e-mail, managers and remote workers need to learn how to conduct effective audio meetings, and to balance e-mail, voice mail conferencing, and face-to-face communications. It is important to plan more formally for regular communications, because people will be working according to different time schedules, and often in different time zones as well.

IMPLICATIONS FOR ORGANIZATIONAL BEHAVIOR

Virtual work environments present a variety of challenges to traditional assumptions about behavior in organizations. For example, when a firm employs teleworkers, what does the concept of absenteeism mean? Is it even relevant, if workers are judged on results? How do such arrangements affect constructs like job satisfaction (a multi-dimensional attitude) and commitment to an organization? How do virtual working arrangements change the construct of performance? These questions remain largely unexplored and unanswered.

No less important are changes in organizational structures and the emergence of new forms of organizations, for example modular organizations, in which a firm focuses on a few core competencies, those it does best—such as designing and marketing computers or copiers—and outsources everything else to a network of suppliers (Spee, 1995; Tully, 1993). In order to work effectively, however, modular organizations need to collaborate smoothly with suppliers, for they will be entrusting them with trade secrets. Modular organizations and virtual organizations are here to stay. They pose a rich agenda of research questions for our field.

REFERENCES

Aannestad, B. & Hooper, J. (1997) The future of groupware in the interactive workplace. *HRMagazine*, **November**: 37–42.
Babbage, C. (1832) *On the Economy of Machinery and Manufactures*. London: Charles Knight.
Bell, D. (1972) Three technologies: size, measurement, hierarchy. In L. E. Davis and J. C. Taylor (Eds), *Design of Jobs*. London: Penguin.
Cascio, W. F. (1996) Managing for maximum performance. *HRMonthly* (Australia), **September**: 10–13.
Cascio, W. F. (1998) The virtual workplace: a reality now. *The Industrial–Organizational Psychologist*, **35** (4): 32–36.
Clark, K. (1997) Home is where the work is. *Fortune*, **November 24**: 219–221.
Gersick, C. J. G. & Davis-Sacks, M. L. (1990) Summary: Task forces. In J. R. Hackman (Ed.), *Groups That Work (and Those That Don't)*. San Francisco: Jossey-Bass, pp. 146–153.
Gupta, Y., Karimi, J. & Somers, T. M. (1995) Telecommuting: problems associated with communications technologies and their capabilities. *IEEE Transactions on Engineering Management*, **42** (4): 305–318.
Hackman, J. R. (Ed.) (1990) *Groups That Work (and Those That Don't)*. San Francisco: Jossey-Bass.
Ishii, H., Kobayashi, M. & Arita, K. (1994) Interactive design of seamless collaboration media. *Communications of the ACM*, **37** (8): 83–97.
Jackson, M. (1997) Telecommuters love staying away, new survey shows. *The Denver Post*, **November 21**: p. 4C.
Kerr, S. (1995) In S. Sherman (Ed.) Stretch goals: the dark side of asking for miracles. *Fortune*, **November 13**: 31.
Matthes, K. (1992) Telecommuting: balancing business and employee needs. *HR Focus*, **December, 69** (3): 3.
Moravec, M. (1996) Bringing performance management out of the stone-age. *Management Review*, **February**: 38–42.
O'Connell, S. E. (1996) The virtual workplace moves at warp speed. *HRMagazine*, **March**: 51–77.
Office hoteling isn't as inn as futurists once thought (1997) *The Wall Street Journal*, **September 2**: p. A1.
Power gizmos to power business (1997) *Business Week*, **November 24**: 190.
Smith, A. (1776) *An Inquiry into the Nature and Causes of the Wealth of Nations (1776)*. In R. H. Campbell, A. S. Skinner & W. B. Todd (Eds), London: Oxford University Press.
Spee, J. C. (1995) Addition by subtraction: outsourcing strengthens business focus. *HRMagazine*, **March**: 38–43.
The new workplace (1996) *Business Week*, **April 29**: 105–113.
Tully, S. (1993) The modular corporation. *Fortune*, **February 8**: 106–108; 112–114.
Wall, T. D., Kemp, N. J., Jackson, P. R. & Clegg, C. W. (1986) Outcomes of autonomous work groups: a long-term field experiment. *Academy of Management Journal*, **29**: 280–304.
Warner, M. (1997) Working at home—the right way to be a star in your bunny slippers. *Fortune*, **March 3**: 165, 166.

CHAPTER 2

The Virtual Organization: Promises and Payoffs, Large and Small

Charles C. Snow
The Smeal College of Business Administration,
The Pennsylvania State University, USA

and

Jessica Lipnack and Jeffrey Stamps
NetAge Inc., Massachusetts, USA

INTRODUCTION

"Just another management fad—or a vision of the future?" That was the question posed by *Business Week* in its 1993 cover story on "The Virtual Corporation" (Byrne, Brandt & Port, 1993). In the ensuing years, numerous books and articles were written about the virtual organization, providing examples that ranged from small bakeries to large oil firms. Whether fad or vision, the virtual organization clearly is a subject of considerable interest as the 21st century dawns. Our own view, based on both research and consulting experience, is that the virtual organization is a viable means of organizing that has produced substantial company and individual benefits. Moreover, the virtual form of organizing promises to provide further payoffs in the future if certain barriers can be overcome. In this Chapter, we offer an overview of the virtual organization: what it is, where it came from, its uses and benefits, and its future research needs.

Trends in Organizational Behavior, Volume 6. Edited by C. L. Cooper and D. M. Rousseau.
Copyright © 1999 John Wiley & Sons, Ltd.

FOUR AGES OF ORGANIZATION

Why are virtual organizations appearing in such variety and profusion? The magnitude of the change now gripping us all—in speed, complexity, and globalization—is captured by the view that humanity is currently undergoing an evolutionary transition from an industrial to an information-based economy and society. However one divides the great epochs of human history, it is apparent we are living through a major paradigm shift. Toffler (1990) uses three "waves of change" to describe the essence of the evolution of human civilization.

Toffler's three waves of change conveniently divide all of human history into four great ages. To span the full range of human organizational capabilities, we need to include the first era. The Nomadic Age, beginning indistinctly between two and three million years ago, was when our ancestors acquired the ability to speak, make tools, and configure social organizations. Populations were sparse and families were relatively small. The Agricultural Age (first wave) began 10–12,000 years ago and marked a dramatic shift from the Nomadic Era. Farming and herding eventually replaced hunting and gathering. Populations grew larger, cities and towns developed, and family size increased as people settled down. The Industrial Age (second wave), running roughly from the 18th through the mid-20th century, saw factories replace farms as the primary economic engine. Populations exploded and urbanized, while families grew smaller. This age represents today's tradition, the old way from which the new seeks to emerge. The Information Age is growing out of the third wave of change, beginning in the latter half of the 20th century. We are now riding the turbulence of transition. The world's economies are becoming information-based, electronically connected, and globally interdependent. Population continues to rise, but families are still small though more diverse.

Each of the great ages also has been the forebear to a new social config-uration (Lipnack & Stamps, 1994: 12–13). Nomads roamed around in small groups. The great agricultural organizations were the first hier-archies. The rise of industrialism brought the large-scale use of bu-reaucracies. The Information Age has its emblematic organization as well: boundary-spanning networks, or virtual organizations. While we do not yet know what term will finally apply to the emergent organization in the Information Age (e.g., network or virtual), we do know that some new form is shaping our future in terms of how and where we work.

Over the ages, we have accumulated organizational knowledge rather than discarded it. When hierarchy came along, people did not stop meeting in small groups. When bureaucracy evolved, hierarchs did not throw down their scepters and call it a day. Indeed, industrial bureaucracies depend upon the ranks and levels that agrarian hierarchies invented. While developing its own signature characteristics, each age also incorporates essential organizational features of the ones before it (Miles et al., 1997).

Various types of networks, the emerging virtual organization of the Information Age, incorporate aspects of their predecessors: the levels of hierarchies, the specialities of bureaucracy, and the purpose of small groups. Old forms do not, however, persist unchanged. With each new age, new versions of old forms supplement the human organizational repertoire. The original autonomous small group—the family—survives today, still central to society yet somewhat different in each era. New forms of hierarchy (e.g., shared leadership at the top) and bureaucracy (e.g., decentralized) are appearing within networked virtual organizations (Miles & Snow, 1994). There is also a new variant on small groups—virtual teams. Thus, the impact of virtual organization is seen at every level as the strains of transition produce a variety of new organizational forms.

WHAT IS A VIRTUAL ORGANIZATION?

As an organizational metaphor, the virtual concept is a product of the Information Age generally and the computer industry in particular. In the early days of computing, "virtual memory" described a way of making a computer act as if it had more storage capacity than it really possessed (Byrne, 1993a). Similarly, early characterizations of the virtual organization suggested that it was more than it appeared to be or that it could do more than its apparent capabilities would allow. Thus, from the very beginning, the virtual organization has had an aura of mystery and power.

Of the several meanings of the word virtual, the one that is most relevant to organizations is "almost". That is, if we normally consider an organization to be a group of collocated individuals, then the virtual organization is almost an organization. However, as noted above, almost does not mean "less than"—indeed, the virtual organization is usually described as something "more than" an organization or at least "different from" the usual organization. The key factors that we believe set a virtual organization apart are that its members work across space, time, and organizational boundaries (Lipnack & Stamps, 1997). Using these three factors as differentiating criteria, virtual organizations can be defined as those that are *multisite, multiorganizational,* and *dynamic.* The main uses, benefits, and cases of the virtual organization, as discussed in academic and practitioner writings, are summarized in Table 2.1.

Table 2.1   Uses, benefits, cases, and studies of virtual organizations

Uses and benefits	Case	Study
A. Multisite Offer a product or service through electronic channels • World Wide Web • Market choice box • TV shopping • Dedicated database (e.g., APOLLO, SABRE) • Proprietary technology (e.g., Electronic Education Environment (E³)) Combine the efforts of geo-graphically dispersed people • Groupware • Video conferencing • E-mail • Ubiquitous computing • Trust building Increase professional lifestyle flexibility • Telecommuting • Self-management	High school University Global consulting firm	Alexander (1997) Benjamin & Wigand (1995) Chellapa, et al. (1997) Cohen (1997) Crandall & Wallace (1997) Dess, et al. (1995) Handy (1995) Hardwick & Bolton (1997) Hiltz (1994) Kostner (1994) Lipnack & Stamps (1997) Moshowitz (1986, 1994, 1997) Nohria & Berkley (1994) Upton & McAfee (1996) Wildstrom (1997)
B. Multiorganizational Focus on core competencies by outsourcing non-core competencies Form close relationships with suppliers to increase efficiency • Supply-chain management processes • Electronic data interchange (EDI) systems Incorporate customers' preferences into your own operations • Intercompany teams • Beta sites Tap into partners' knowledge and expertise	Bakery Entertainment company Computer firm High school	Alexander (1997) Bleecker (1994) Byrne, et al. (1993) Chesbrough & Teece (1996) Crandall & Wallace (1997) Davidow & Malone (1992) Davis & Darling (1995, 1996) Dess, et al. (1995) Faucheux (1997) Goldman, et al. (1995) Hardwick, et al. (1996) Hardwick & Bolton (1997) Lipnack & Stamps (1997) Moshowitz (1994, 1997) Nohria & Berkley (1994) O'Leary, et al. (1997) Upton & McAfee (1996) Voss (1996) Wildstrom (1997)
C. Dynamic Perform tasks quickly Change partners and/or relationships frequently Use time as a strategic resource		Byrne, et al. (1993) Chesbrough & Teece (1996) Crandall & Wallace (1997) Davidow & Malone (1992) Goldman, et al. (1995) Hardwick & Bolton (1997) Lipnack & Stamps (1997) Moshowitz (1994, 1997) O'Leary, et al. (1997) Voss (1996)

USES AND BENEFITS OF VIRTUAL ORGANIZATIONS

Organizations noted for having all three characteristics (multisite, multiorganizational, dynamic) began to appear in the 1970s and spread rapidly throughout the next two decades. Of course, many traditional organizations of that time operated with multiple locations. However, as part of the globalization process that was earnestly underway, new company locations were often international. Not only was the new facility geographically distant, but probably it was culturally distant as well. Operating effectively across geographic and cultural space required many companies to rethink how they managed people and other resources. One major outgrowth of this process was an increased emphasis on the use of transnational teams coupled with advanced means of electronic communication and decision making (Kostner, 1994; Snow *et al.*, 1996).

During the 1980s and even into the 1990s, many American companies in particular began to depart from the traditional competitive notion of "do everything yourself". One striking case of an old, large company in rapid transition is Shell Oil Company. Facing severe economic difficulties in the early 1990s, Shell in 1994 took its first major step towards virtualization—the disaggregation of its hierarchical structure. Since network organizations consist of nodes, each of which has a significant degree of independence and freedom of action, Shell first reformed its bureaucratic structure into four business units, each with its own President, Board of Directors, and profit responsibility (Exploration and Production, Oil Products, Chemicals, and Services).

As Shell was devolving internally, it was caught in an external web of powerful global market forces. One trend within the larger Royal Dutch/ Shell Group was to integrate globally along business lines. Therefore, components of both Shell U.S. Chemicals and Services became part of a Royal Dutch/Shell network serving global customers who were similarly distributed. The second major trend was in retailing, the downstream end of the business. Here Shell formed a number of joint ventures and alliances, including some with competitors such as Texaco and Amoco. These changes have radically reshaped Shell Oil as a company. As recently as 1995, nearly 100 per cent of Shell's capital was employed in Shell-owned companies. Today, only a little more than one-third of its capital is in wholly-owned enterprises. Almost half of Shell's capital has been committed to joint ventures, while another 16 per cent is in various global alliances with the Royal Dutch/Shell Group.

Disaggregating hierarchical organizations through outsourcing and partnering, as Shell has done, is now commonplace, as companies increasingly choose to develop their business strategies tightly around their core competencies (Prahalad & Hamel, 1990). Partnerships and alliances of various sorts—with suppliers, major customers, and other companies—are regularly used to obtain needed expertise, gain access to distribution channels and markets, lower costs, and so on (Johnston & Lawrence, 1988). Heavy use of partnering and outsourcing has resulted in the creation of multifirm value chains that, in order to be effective, must be well managed. Eventually, a given company's managers realize that the "organization" which they are managing is not only their own but also includes boundary-spanning relationships with other firms along the company's value chain. Such a multifirm organization has been called, variously, the modular corporation (Tully, 1993), horizontal corporation (Byrne, 1993b), network organization (Lipnack & Stamps, 1982, 1993; Miles & Snow, 1986), and industry value chain (Porter, 1985). The critical managerial competence required by a multifirm network is collaboration, and the most visible American example of such a managerial approach is General Electric's Work-Out program in which the company's managers, along with key suppliers, customers, and partners, work together to simplify and improve business processes (Ashkenas et al., 1995; Tichy & Charan, 1989).

In addition to being multisite and multiorganizational, some of the newer network organizations are also very dynamic—they are used temporarily for a particular purpose and then reconfigured for the next project. Such organizations, because of their speed and flexibility, can use time as a strategic resource and compete by developing time-based strategies (Stalk & Hout, 1990). The mantra of the dynamic network organization is "anything, anytime, anywhere," and these organizations are dedicated to conducting their business efficiently, effectively, and quickly. The company that is perhaps most recognized for its dynamic organizational abilities is Dell Computer. It has long been a model of just-in-time manufacturing and assembly, but now is also regarded as among the best in inventory and purchasing management, logistics, order-to-cash conversion, and doing business on the Internet (Brown, 1997; Mc-Williams, 1997). It is a dynamic network such as that operated by Dell that is most often referred to as a virtual organization (Magretta, 1998).

As has been the case with all new organizational forms, the virtual organization has produced its own unique managerial roles (Miles & Snow, 1994). Because it is essentially a horizontal rather than vertical (hierarchical) organization, the virtual organization's operating effectiveness is highly dependent on managers who can collaborate both within and across organizational boundaries. For example, virtual organization *designers* rely on their conceptual and partnering skills to conceive and construct multiorganizational networks. Network *co-operators* use their negotiating and contracting skills to hook together firms in alliances of varying duration to perform projects. And, because networks require continual enhancement if they are to operate smoothly and effectively, managers who play the *developer* role engage in a variety of actions that help the network to learn and improve.

In many international companies, both large and small, these three managerial roles form the core of a virtual team—a geographically dispersed group of individuals who use a variety of electronic technologies to regularly perform cross-boundary work (Lipnack & Stamps, 1997). Virtual organizations of the future increasingly will be composed of such teams.

WHAT IS A VIRTUAL TEAM?

Over thousands of years, human life has spawned many kinds of small groups. What is common to all types of groups? Can we identify a generic small group with a few salient and theoretically important characteristics? To see what is special about teams we need to understand what is common to all small groups. Then we can distinguish virtual teams from other kinds of teams.

As recently as the mid-1980s, the standard theoretical model of small groups was a loose composite of scattered research in anthropology, sociology, organizational psychology, and management. At that time, there was a building consensus that a small group was a coherent system that one could study independently at the crossroads of several disciplines, but it was not a well-developed field. A decade later, after much empirical testing in both field and laboratory settings, the standard model's definition of a small group held up well: "Virtually all definitions of the term *small group* include three attributes: two or more individuals, interaction among group members, and interdependence among them in some way" (Guzzo *et al.*, 1995). This leads to our own concise characterization of a small group as "individuals interacting interdependently".

The standard model of a small group embeds it in a larger context. It is rare that a new small group arises out of nowhere. Usually, small groups arise from pre-existing groups—the special accounts group that emerges from within the finance department, the book club that is adjunctive to the church, the pick-up basketball team that grows out of the playground-building project. In business, small groups are invariably part of a larger organization or set of organizations.

Individuals

Individual members of the group define its boundaries. Whatever it is that enables people to say they are "in" the group while others are "out" of the group identifies the boundary. When people are on an e-mail distribution list, they establish themselves as members of that virtual group. If you are not on the list, you are not a member. Membership recognized by insiders and outsiders alike gives a group one of its basic boundaries.

Interactions

The second element of a small group is interaction, the multiple links among its members. Communication, the foundation for human interaction and relationships, is inherently a shared activity. Language, first invented in the earliest forager camps, continues to be concocted in new groups today. Acronyms, jargon, and in-jokes are all linguistic indicators of group cohesion. For millennia, small group communications meant that people talked to one another face-to-face, using the medium of sound waves travelling in air. Today, that is changing, with an ever-increasing array of non-face-to-face technologies becoming available. We are experiencing the most dramatic change in the nature of the small group since humans acquired the capacity to talk to one another.

Interdependence

Researchers prefer the term "interdependence" to describe what most popular writers refer to as "unifying purpose" or "shared goals". The words "individuals interacting" are not sufficient to define a small group. There must be interdependence, a mutual purpose and shared motivation that incorporate individuals into a group whole.

From Groups To Teams

Using the standard model, the step from small groups to teams is straightforward. Both the research literature and the popular press express the distinction in the same way: "Teams exist for some task-oriented purpose" (Guzzo et al., 1995: 115). The orientation to task is what distinguishes teams from other types of small groups such as families, social groups, and governing bodies. While all small groups carry out tasks to some degree (as well as make decisions and support social interactions), task is the primary focus for teams. All other factors are secondary.

While the task focus helps to distinguish teams from small groups, the essential characteristic of *virtual* teams is the boundary-crossing nature of their interactions. The day-to-day reality of communicating, interacting, and forming relationships across space, time, and organizations makes teams virtual.

USES AND BENEFITS OF VIRTUAL TEAMS

Buckman Laboratories is a sea of virtual teams that constantly form and disband (Lipnack & Stamps, 1997). To address a customer's problem or request, a global virtual team comes together without anyone chartering it, and the team includes anyone in the company who chooses to particip-ate on a particular project. When the project is over, the virtual team disbands. Buckman's teams are quite different from traditional task groups comprising people from the same organization working in the same place at the same time.

Since we are in new territory here with a new type of team, we need some coordinates to explore the terrain. One point of reference is the familiar one of space and time. *Distributed* teams are composed of people in the same organization who work in different places, either inter-dependently (like a multisite product development group), or separately (like branches and local offices). Buckman's research and development operation, for example, is distributed across all of the company's sites. Some of Buckman's teams are especially dynamic. In a dynamic team, people are in constant motion with very complex schedules (like a sales team).

Less obvious but equally important is the dimension of organization. In traditional Industrial Age collocated teams, people work side-by-side (the same space and time) on interdependent tasks for the same organization. Several decades ago, even before the new communications technologies were widely available, one form of virtual team began to appear, the *cross-organizational* team. Today, cross-organizational teams of various kinds are common.

Collocated cross-organizational teams comprise people from different organizations who work together in the same place. Perhaps the most familiar type of virtual team is the classic cross-functional group of ex-perts and stakeholders who come together to solve problems or seize opportunities that require cooperation across organizational boundaries. A good example is the Shell Deepwater Project team that developed the process for designing, building, and running drilling operations and pipelines a mile undersea.

Distributed cross-organizational teams involve people from different organizations who work in different places. An oft-described virtual team combines people in different places and organizations with a need to function at the same time (synchronously). However, most work combines individual and group tasks, time spent working alone and time spent working with others. For most virtual teams, synchronous interaction—shared time—is a scarce resource. Time together is planned, prepared for, and followed-up on. Hewlett-

Packard's worldwide distributed Product Information Management System team combines quarterly face-to-face meetings and extensive use of electronic media to function across global distances and 24-hour time frames.

Time creates a complication that not even instantaneous communication can solve. As the distance increases and more time zones are crossed, the window of synchronicity in the workday narrows. New England is six hours behind Europe, and people in California leave work just as their counterparts start their next day in Japan. Even when real-time interaction is possible technically, it may not be practical. Some virtual teams, such as one mobile telecommunications R&D team at Texas Instruments, have turned this type of situation into an advantage by dividing its members among locations in France, California, and Japan, and then passing work sequentially so that a 24-hour workday is achieved.

The most extreme type of virtual team is one that is cross-organizational and that rarely (in some cases never) meets in the course of doing its work. Without face-to face time, this type of team tests the limits of dealing with contentious issues, but may shine for information-sharing and technical problem-solving tasks. Buckman Laboratories' global conversation system provides conditions that allow worldwide cross-organizational teams to form within hours to work on a customer problem or opportunity that may last for only days or weeks.

When teams go global, their language and cultural issues clearly loom larger. However, all teams of the future will have to cope with the fact of increasing diversity in the workplace. Not only is the workforce becoming more diverse, but the task requirements of complex work demand that a more diverse group of people work together, whether in traditional settings or in virtual teams. Sometimes collocated teams have even greater difficulty than virtual teams dealing with variations in language and culture. Because they are less aware of their communication barriers, collocated teams do not necessarily create appropriate compensatory norms. There is an analogy here to the relationship between distance and collaboration. Data show that people are somewhat less likely to communicate with a colleague upstairs in the same building than with one in another building (Kraut & Egido, 1988). When people know they are at a distance—culturally and linguistically as well as spatially—they are more conscious of the need to be explicit and intentional about communication.

In sum, virtual teams in network organizations have certain advantages over collocated teams in traditional organizations. When properly composed and surrounded with appropriate infrastructure, such teams provide enormous benefits of speed, flexibility, and access to knowledge.

FUTURE RESEARCH NEEDS

Returning to Table 2.1, it is apparent that the literature specifically addressing virtual teams and organizations has three main characteristics: (1) it is very new (most citations are from the 1990s); (2) it is more conceptual than empirical; and (3) the limited amount of empirical research conducted to date consists mostly of descriptive case studies. Therefore, the agenda for future research on this topic is unlimited. We offer the following recommendations for those who are interested in conducting research on virtual teams and organizations.

(1) *Identify the various information technologies found in virtual organizations and investigate how they are used.* Virtual organizations are heavy users of electronically-based information technologies. They use such technologies to communicate, store data, and make decisions. However, they increasingly use information technologies to create and develop markets (e.g., amazon.com on the Internet) and to leverage knowledge assets (e.g., Arthur Andersen, Skandia, and other companies' attempts to build knowledge-management systems). We need contingency models that link particular technologies and situations, and we need descriptive studies of how information-technology systems can create value both internally and externally. Key contingency factors are the multisite, multiorganizational, and dynamic dimensions of the virtual organization.

(2) *Study virtual teams in order to understand and improve large virtual organizations.* A microcosm of large-scale virtual organizations can be found in multisite, multiorganizational, and dynamic virtual teams. Indeed, the activities of large virtual organizations are performed by teams that form among parts of the cooperating organizations. An alliance between big companies, for example, is usually formed by a few senior people from the prospective partners, then implementation is executed by small cross-boundary groups drawn from several levels of the respective organizations. Virtual teams are also the practical level for most empirical studies, particularly those research efforts that include the human factors that are essential to understanding the nature of this newer group form.

(3) *Construct change models that help managers transform hierarchical organizations into virtual organizations.* As just noted, virtual "organizations" are often a group of teams that span traditional hierarchical organizations. In order to create a high-performing virtual organization, therefore, it is usually necessary to first change hierarchical processes. Years of experience with business process reengineering have taught us how to perform this step. However, reengineering

primarily helps an organization become more efficient; it does not specify the new relationships and processes that must be put in place to operate a virtual organization. Virtual teams and organizations are composed of partners with complementary expertise, who trust one another to make high-quality contributions in a timely way, and who collectively endorse a continuous-improvement philosophy. In our experience, the key leverage points in changing a hierarchical system to a virtual system are the following: (a) instilling a "human invest-ment" management philosophy within and around the virtual organization/team so that people can essentially manage themselves (Miles & Snow, 1994: Chapter 9); (b) developing a "learning organiza-tion" culture and infrastructure to facilitate adaptation (Senge, 1990); (c) realigning reward systems and creating internal entrepreneurial processes to promote the vigorous pursuit of business objectives (Pinchot & Pinchot, 1993); and (d) engaging in team-building ac-tivities to develop strong group processes under virtual conditions (Lipnack & Stamps, 1997; Snow et al., 1996).

(4) *Develop multiple effectiveness measures for changes from traditional to vir-tual models.* There are no agreed-upon, universal measures of organ-izational success. Researchers usually can choose an "internal" measure of effectiveness such as the virtual team meeting its own goals. However, even more important are "external" measures that link the team's efforts to the firm's competitive strategy and its broader multiorganizational objectives. Even traditional time frames for measuring success are likely to be different since virtual organiza-tions typically are able to act faster than hierarchical organizations. For practitioners, measuring the effectiveness of a change effort should begin with a formal "Case for Action" for the transformation process that describes why a virtual organization is necessary and how performance will be measured at the team, company, and net-work organization levels. To build our knowledge in this area, it is important to relate the circumstances and measures to the key dimen-sions of the virtual organization being examined—multisite, multi-organizational, and/or dynamic.

(5) *Study the relationship between social capital and business success.* Social capital accumulates as people work together—it is the value of the relationships in an organization (Coleman, 1988). Virtual organiza-tions have the potential to create different forms of social capital than those produced by traditional organizations. For example, because of their heavy reliance on external partners, virtual organizations can create valuable relationships that cut across companies, core compe-tencies, and even entire industries. Social capital raised through part-nering can be used to gain deeper and wider access to technologies

and markets. Also, because virtual organizations compress time and space, social capital can be quickly amassed (or lost) across great distances. Thus, to the extent that social capital can be used to fuel business development, virtual organizations appear to be in a more powerful position than hierarchical organizations. Studies of what types of social capital are associated with business development and success, as well as how the process occurs, will be especially important to understanding global business in the 21st century.

CONCLUSIONS

The virtual organization—vision or fad? Although the rigorous research is limited, it seems clear that the virtual organization is not a fad. As we have discussed in this Chapter, the virtual organization is essentially a network organization. A given company develops its competitive strategy around its particular core competencies and then searches for partners whose expertise and resources are needed to complete the product or service offering. When the network of partners is spread across large geographic areas, and when relationships change frequently, the organization is considered to be virtual. The network or virtual mode of organizing has been used heavily since at least the 1980s.

In several important ways, the virtual organization appears to be ideally suited for today's business environment. For example, it relies on internal as well as external market mechanisms to make decisions and allocate resources. As more and more countries make the transition to free-enterprise economies, the virtual organization promises to provide a better fit than hierarchical organizations. Virtual organizations also tend to provide more autonomy for their members and more opportunities for them to practice their professional specialties. For example, telecommuting and other forms of autonomy are common in multisite situations, and virtual teams that include representatives of other firms typically have more respect and influence than do teams that are wholly contained inside traditional organizations. Lastly, because virtual organizations may regularly change their network of partners and/or their operating procedures, those organizations are better able to deal with the hypercompetitive conditions found in many industries today than are their hierarchical counterparts.

Of course, there are significant barriers that some companies will have to overcome if they wish to operate effective virtual teams and organizations. Prominent among these barriers are managerial philosophies that do not allow for large amounts of member influence and autonomy, and reward systems that prevent members from sharing in or owning their

.ccomplishments. All too often, the difficulties of human communication, institutional inertia, and people's reluctance to change, together with limits to the still-evolving technologies supporting cross-boundary collaboration, impair the effectiveness of virtual organizations. However, in the long evolution of organizational forms, the virtual organization is solidly in place and likely to remain in the forefront of practice well into the 21st century.

REFERENCES

Alexander, M. (1997) Getting to grips with the virtual organization. *Long Range Planning*, **30**: 122–124.

Ashkenas, R., Ulrich, D., Jick, T. & Kerr, S. (1995) *The Boundaryless Organization: Breaking the Chains of Organizational Structure*. San Francisco: Jossey-Bass.

Benjamin, R. & Wigand, R. (1995) Electronic markets and virtual value chains on the information superhighway. *Sloan Management Review*, **36**: 62–72.

Bleecker, S. (1994) The virtual organization. *The Futurist*, **28**: 9–14.

Brown, E. (1997) Could the very best PC maker be Dell Computer? *Fortune*, **April 14**: 26–27.

Byrne, J. A. (1993a) The futurists who fathered the ideas. *Business Week*, **February 8**: 41.

Byrne, J. A. (1993b) The horizontal corporation. *Business Week*, **December 20**: 76–81.

Byrne, J. A., Brandt, R. & Port, O. (1993) The virtual corporation. *Business Week*, **February 8**: 36–40.

Chellapa, R., Barua, A. & Whinston, A. B. (1997) An electronic infrastructure for a virtual university. *Communications of the ACM*, **40**: 56–58.

Chesbrough, H. W. & Teece, D. J. (1996) When is virtual virtuous? Organizing for innovation. *Harvard Business Review*, **74**: 65–73.

Cohen, S. (1997) On becoming virtual. *Training & Development*, **51**: 30–37.

Coleman, J. S. (1988) Social capital in the creation of human capital. *American Journal of Sociology*, **94** (Supplement): 95–120.

Crandall, N. F. & Wallace, M. J., Jr. (1997) Inside the virtual workplace: forging a new deal for work and rewards. *Compensation & Benefits Review*, **29**: 27–36.

Davidow, W. H. & Malone, M. S. (1992) *The Virtual Corporation: Structuring and Revitalizing the Corporation for the 21st Century*. New York: Harper Business.

Davis, T. R. V. & Darling, B. L. (1995) How virtual corporations manage the performance of contractors: the Super Bakery case. *Organizational Dynamics*, **24**: 70–75.

Davis, T. R. V. & Darling, B. L. (1996) ABC in a virtual corporation. *Management Accounting*, **78**: 18–26.

Dess, G. G., Rasheed, A. M. A., McLaughlin, K. J. & Priem, R. L. (1995) The new corporate architecture. *Academy of Management Executive*, **9**: 7–18.

Faucheux, C. (1997) How virtual organizing is transforming management science. *Communications of the ACM*, **40**, 50–55.

Goldman, S. L., Nagel, R. N. & Preiss, K. (1995) *Agile Competitors and Virtual Organizations: Strategies for Enriching the Customer*. New York: Van Nostrand Reinhold.

Guzzo, R. A., Salas, E. and Associates (1995) *Team Effectiveness and Decision Making in Organizations*. San Francisco: Jossey-Bass.

Handy, C. (1995) Trust and virtual organization: how do you manage people whom you do not see? *Harvard Business Review*, **73**: 40–50.

Hardwick, M. & Bolton, R. (1997) The industrial virtual enterprise. *Communications of the ACM*, **40**: 59–60.

Hardwick, M., Spooner, D., Rando, T. & Morris, K. C. (1996) Sharing manufacturing information in virtual enterprises. *Communications of the ACM*, **39**: 46–54.

Hiltz, S. R. (1994) *The Virtual Classroom: Learning without Limits via Computer Networks*, Norwood, NJ: Ablex.

Johnston, R. & Lawrence, P. R. (1988) Beyond vertical integration—the rise of the value-adding partnership. *Harvard Business Review*, **66**: 94–101.

Kostner, J. (1994) *Virtual Leadership: Secrets from the Round Table for the Multi-site Manager*. New York: Warner Books.

Kraut, R. & Egido, C. (1988) Patterns of contact and communication in scientific research collaboration. *Computer-Supported Cooperative Work Conference Proceedings*. New York: Association for Computing Machinery.

Lipnack, J. & Stamps, J. (1982) *Networking: The First Report and Directory*. New York: Doubleday & Company.

Lipnack, J. & Stamps, J. (1993) *The TeamNet Factor: Bringing the Power of Boundary Crossing Into the Heart of Your Business*. Essex Junction, VT: Oliver Wight Publications.

Lipnack, J. & Stamps, J. (1994) *The Age of the Network: Organizing Principles for the 21st Century*. Essex Junction, VT: Oliver Wight Publications.

Lipnack, J. & Stamps, J. (1997) *Virtual Teams: Reaching Across Space, Time, and Organizations with Technology*. New York: John Wiley & Sons.

Magretta, J. (1998) The power of virtual integration: an interview with Dell Computer's Michael Dell. *Harvard Business Review*, **76**: 72–84.

McWilliams, G. (1997) Whirlwind on the web. *Business Week*, **April 7**: 132–136.

Miles, R. E. & Snow, C. C. (1986) Organizations: new concepts for new forms. *California Management Review*, **28**: 62–73.

Miles, R. E. & Snow, C. C. (1994) *Fit, Failure, and the Hall of Fame: How Companies Succeed or Fail*. New York: Free Press.

Miles, R. E., Snow, C. C., Mathews, J. A., Miles, G. & Coleman, H. J., Jr. (1997) Organizing in the knowledge age: anticipating the cellular form. *Academy of Management Executive*, **11**: 7–20.

Moshowitz, A. (1986) Social dimensions of office automation. In M. C. Yovits (Ed.), *Advances in Computers*. Volume 25, pp. 335–404. New York: Academic Press.

Moshowitz, A. (1994) Virtual organization: a vision of management in the information age. *Information Society*, **10**: 267–288.

Moshowitz, A. (1997) Virtual organization. *Communications of the ACM*, **40**: 30–37.

Nohria, N. & Berkley, J. D. (1994) The virtual organization: bureaucracy, technology, and the implosion of control. In C. Heckscher and A. Donnellon (Eds), *The Post-Bureaucratic Organization: New Perspectives on Organizational Change*, pp. 108–128. Thousand Oaks, CA: Sage Publications.

O'Leary, D. E., Kuokka, D. & Plant, R. (1997) Artificial intelligence and virtual organizations. *Communications of the ACM*, **40**: 52–59.

Pinchot, G. & Pinchot, E. (1993) *The End of Bureaucracy and the Rise of the Intelligent Organization*. San Francisco: Berrett-Koehler.

Porter, M. E. (1985) *Competitive Advantage*. New York: Free Press.

Prahalad, C. K. & Hamel, G. (1990) The core competence of the corporation. *Harvard Business Review*, **68**: 79–91.

Senge, P. M. (1990) *The Fifth Discipline: The Art & Practice of the Learning Organization.* New York: Doubleday.

Snow, C. C., Snell, S. A., Canney Davison, S. & Hambrick, D. C. (1996) Use transnational teams to globalize your company. *Organizational Dynamics,* **24**: 50–67.

Stalk, G., Jr. & Hout, T. M. (1990) *Competing Against Time: How Time-Based Competition Is Reshaping Global Markets.* New York: Free Press.

Tichy, N. & Charan, R. (1989) Speed, simplicity, self-confidence: an interview with Jack Welch. *Harvard Business Review,* **67**: 112–120.

Toffler, A. (1990) *The Third Wave.* New York: William Morrow and Company.

Tully, S. (1993) The modular corporation. *Fortune,* **February 8**: 106–114.

Upton, D. M. & McAfee, A. (1996) The real virtual factory. *Harvard Business Review,* **74**: 123–133.

Voss, H. (1996) Virtual organization. *Strategy and Leadership,* **24**: 12–24.

Wildstrom, S. H. (1997) The world-wide classroom. *Business Week,* **December 29**: 18.

CHAPTER 3

Managers in a Virtual Context: The Experience of Self-threat and its Effects on Virtual Work Organizations

Batia M. Wiesenfeld
New York University, USA

Sumita Raghuram
Fordham University, USA

and

Raghu Garud
New York University, USA

INTRODUCTION

Virtual work programs are proliferating rapidly in organizations all over the world. To date, however, relatively little research exists to help organizations understand and manage virtual employees. The research that does exist generally focuses on the experience of virtual workers themselves. For example, research has examined telecommuters' quality of work life (Shamir & Solomon, 1985) and the role of communication in predicting the strength of telecommuters' organizational identification (Wiesenfeld, Raghuram & Garud, 1999, Communication patterns as determinants of organization identification in a virtual organization, forthcoming in *Organization Science*, vol 10, issue 6). Relatively neglected to date is the role that middle managers and supervisors play in the success or failure of a

Trends in Organizational Behavior, Volume 6. Edited by C. L. Cooper and D. M. Rousseau.
Copyright © 1999 John Wiley & Sons, Ltd.

virtual work initiative. We suggest that these managers play a critical role: they may function as an obstacle to the spread of virtual work and their cooperation is essential if virtual work initiatives are to succeed.

Our team has studied the increasingly prevalent phenomena of virtual work over the past four years. These research efforts include numerous interviews, surveys, focus groups, and direct observation in multiple organizational settings. We recently completed a benchmarking study examining 20 different organizations with virtual work programs that range from voluntary to mandatory, high participation to low participation, recently instituted to longstanding, concentrated in particular divisions to widespread throughout the firm. Three anecdotes culled from this research illustrate the importance of managers to the success or failure of virtual work initiatives.

First, in our early interviews of virtual workers, we noted that the degree to which employees were satisfied and productive as telecommuters seemed to be closely related to whether or not their supervisors were also virtual. Specifically, those virtual workers who were supervised by managers who also telecommute were more likely to feel trusted, reported being more satisfied and more productive, and were less likely to feel that their virtual status would have a negative impact on their career progress. In contrast, employees whose supervisors were desked (i.e., who worked from traditional, centralized offices) were less satisfied, more likely to consider returning to the office full-time, and more likely to expect that telecommuting would have a negative impact on their careers.

A second source of evidence emerges from conversations with telecommuters who were very happy and productive as virtual workers but were forced to return to traditional, centralized offices at the request of their supervisor. Given the choice, these individuals would have continued to telecommute indefinitely, and felt resentful and angry that they were asked to return to the office. In some cases, this resentment was powerful enough that they left the job rather than return to traditional offices. In these instances, due to the attitudes of their managers, not only were these employees lost to the virtual work program but they were also lost to the organization entirely.

A third telling anecdote occurred during a conference attended by individuals whose job responsibilities involved spearheading virtual work initiatives in their organizations. These virtual work coordinators reported that the primary obstacle to the expansion of virtual work programs in their organizations is the resistance of middle managers—those who must supervise virtual employees. According to the virtual work coordinators, the resistance of middle managers lowers the rate at which employees participate in, and hinders the success of, virtual work initiatives.

These observations suggest that the attitudes and behaviors of managers may be an important factor explaining variance in the growth and success of virtual work initiatives (DeSanctis, 1984). The present paper explores how managers experience and react to virtual work. Our goal is to map out directions for future research that explicitly acknowledge the role of managers in the success or failure of virtual work initiatives.

MANAGERS' RESISTANCE TO VIRTUAL WORK

According to a recent benchmarking study, virtual work initiatives are often welcomed by employees, frequently lower costs (such as real estate expenses) for organizations, and if anything have a positive impact on worker productivity (Garud & Dunbar, 1998). Why, then, would managers be likely to resist virtual work?

To understand managers' experiences in a virtual context, it is essential to understand how virtual work alters the organization as a whole. Virtual work has the capacity to change not only the location where work is performed but also some of the most fundamental aspects of organizations, including organizational form (Garud & Lucas, 1998, "Virtual organizations and information technology: a design for fast response," manuscript under editorial review; Miles & Snow, 1986). Whereas traditional organizations may be best characterized as hierarchies (Williamson, 1991), virtual organizations may require a different structure and governance system. Although it is increasingly clear that traditional organizational forms may not be well suited to the virtual context, it is not yet clear what form virtual organizations will take. One possibility is that virtual organizations may be changing from hierarchies to heterarchies or network organizations (Garud & Lucas, 1998; Miles & Snow, 1986; Nohria & Eccles, 1992, Powell, 1990).

With uncertainty and change in organizational form, employees are likely to perceive that their organization's identity is undergoing change. Of particular relevance to this paper, these new organizational forms necessitate new governance structures, creating ambiguity about the role of managers. Ambiguity or change in the organizational identity and governance structures may threaten managers' identification with the organization in general and with their managerial role in particular.

Departure from the traditional hierarchical organizational form may erode longstanding status structures—the same status structures that privileged managers. With their status eroding, managers may experience some loss of esteem. Furthermore, hierarchical structures conferred power and authority on managers, implicitly rewarding the "command-and-control" style of management. As organizational forms and governance structures change, power and control may be based on different criteria, thus threatening traditional managers' sense of control over outcomes.

In sum, we propose that managers who resist virtual work do so because they experience the changes involved in the transition to a virtual context as a personal threat. Specifically, virtual work potentially threatens critical aspects of a managers' self-concept, including identity, esteem, and managers' sense of control. We suggest that managers' behaviors in reaction to virtual work may be understood as a manifestation of their experience of self-threat, and may possibly represent managers' attempts to restore the self in the face of threats to identity, esteem, or control.

Threats to Identity

Theory suggests that an individuals' identity is composed of a single personal identity and multiple social identities (Turner, 1982). To have a strong identity, individuals' personal and social identities must be clear and consistent. When a person's identity is uncertain or ambiguous, their identity is weakened and the individual may experience identity threat. We argue that attributes of virtual work have the potential to weaken managers' identification with their managerial role and with the organizational identity, thus creating identity threat.

For example, a component of managers' identity is their identification with their managerial role, and this managerial role may change or become less clear as a result of virtual work. In particular, because many managers are not responsible for completing specific tasks but rather for supervising others, the key sources of information defining their managerial identity may be symbolic. For instance, managers in traditional organizations may see a room full of their subordinates as one indicator of their managerial identity. The type of office they have (i.e., its size, positioning, and furnishings) may be another symbolic cue.

The symbolic cues that provide information about an individual's managerial identity may be different or entirely absent in a virtual organization, thus creating uncertainty or ambiguity. For example, in many virtual organizations, employees work at home or on the road rather than at desks outside a manager's office door. Furthermore, corner offices that project the manager's status in face-to-face meetings with subordinates (and others) are no longer sufficiently useful. If managers telecommute themselves, their work context may have none of the symbolic cues of their organizational affiliation, let alone their managerial status. Thus, the symbolic cues that define and strengthen managers' identification with their managerial role are likely to change in a virtual context, whether the manager telecommutes or not. Moreover managers who telecommute may experience even greater weakening of their organizational identification than managers who remain in the office.

Another source of identity threat that stems from virtual work is likely to affect non-managers as well as managers, but it may be experienced as more threatening to managers. Specifically, in most modern societies, an individual's organizational identification is a critically important source of social identity (Ashforth & Mael, 1989). The organizational identity is defined as members' perception of the organization's central, enduring, and distinctive character (Dutton & Dukerich, 1991). To have a strong social identity, organization members must have a clear sense of the character of their employing organization and its components (such as departments and work groups). Because members' social identities are linked to the organizational identity, if virtual work weakens the organizational identity, it also has the potential to threaten individuals' social identity.

In traditional organizations, members formulate an understanding of the organizational identity based on various cues. Among these are artifacts, such as architecture, interior design, and standard dress (Dutton, Dukerich & Harquail, 1994; Wiesenfeld, Raghuram & Garud, 1999, Communication patterns as determinants of organizational identification in a virtual organization, forthcoming in *Organization Science*, vol 10, issue 6). Other cues come from the beliefs and behaviors of fellow organization members, frequently transmitted tacitly by individuals who are co-located in centralized offices (Dutton, Dukerich & Harquail, 1994; Raghuram, 1996).

Virtual work, however, may be identity threatening because it weakens the organization's core identity. For example, many of the cues that provide information about the organizational identity (i.e., artifacts and cues from fellow organization members) are less available and less salient when employees are dispersed (Wiesenfeld, Raghuram & Garud, 1999, Communication patterns as determinants of organizational identification in a virtual organization, forthcoming in *Organization Science*, vol 10, issue 6). Furthermore, virtual work initiatives are a form of organizational change. Any form of change may create uncertainty about the organization's enduring character because change alters factors that are symbolic of the organization's values, such as its objectives. The fact that virtual work may profoundly influence organizational form (e.g., creating a transition from a hierarchical to a network structure) may call into question what the organization represents.

Virtual work may also alter employees' expectations about their role in, and future with, the organization. As a result, the changes that accompany virtual work may weaken employees' identities as organization members. In sum, the introduction of virtual work may create uncertainty or change in (a) members' perceptions of the organizational identity, and (b) members' perception of their identity as an organization member—thus threatening individuals' social identity.

These changes and their resulting impact on members' social identity affect all employees, both virtual and non-virtual. However, although all organization members may experience some threat to their social identity as a result of the changes involved in virtual work, this threat is likely to be especially great for individuals with the strongest attachment to, and identification with, the organization. This is true because greater attachment to the organization increases the importance of individuals' organizationally-relevant identities.

Managers may have relatively stronger attachment to and identification with the organization for several reasons (Wiesenfeld & Thibault, 1997, "Managers are employees, too: Exploring the relationships between procedural fairness, managers' self-perceptions, and managerial behaviors following a layoff). For instance, managers' position as leaders of the organization creates the expectation of a strong link between the organization and the manager. Factors (such as longer tenure) that may be correlated with their managerial status may lead managers to have relatively stronger attachment to and identification with the organization. Also, employees who are more strongly identified with the organization may be more likely to be promoted to, or self-select themselves to become, managers (Wiesenfeld & Thibault, 1997). If managers are more strongly identified with the organization and virtual work weakens the organizational identity, managers are likely to experience greater identity threat than other employees.

In sum, virtual work may create uncertainty about, or change in, the organizational identity and the individual's managerial role. As a result, managers' identification with the organization or their role in it may be weakened, and this may be experienced as an identity threat.

Threats to Esteem

Individuals wish to maintain high self-esteem, that is, to evaluate themselves positively.[1] The changes that occur with the institution of a virtual work program may be especially threatening to the self-esteem of managers. Specifically, research suggests that in an organizational context, individuals' sense of self-esteem depends upon feeling that they are important, influential, efficient, and respected (Pierce et al., 1989). Managers

---

[1]Threats to identity and threats to esteem may be difficult to distinguish fully. Social identity theory suggests that individuals wish to maintain a *positive* social identity because individuals' self-evaluations are at least partially dependent upon their evaluations of their membership groups. Thus, the relationship between perceived positivity of one's social identity and the experience of identity threat may be thought of as mediated through self-esteem. For clarity of exposition, our discussion of threats to identity focuses on identity clarity and our discussion of threats to esteem focuses on negative evaluations whether of the self directly or of one's social identity.

receive feedback that tells them how they should evaluate themselves in these respects, and that feedback may change along with the changes involved in virtual work.

Perhaps of greatest significance, the transition to virtual work may involve meaningful change in managers' organizational role. Specifically, if governance structures change as a result of virtual work, then the skills, practices, and attributes that may have been highly valued and effective for managers in a traditional office environment may be difficult to sustain and possibly even detrimental in a virtual work context. If their skills, practices and attributes are no longer valued or useful, managers' sense of self-esteem may be threatened.

For example, consider the role that managers play in supervising their subordinates. In traditional work organizations, managers may be considered effective if they are in frequent contact with subordinates and peers so that they are perceived to be available to them when needed. Also, many managers employ supervisory techniques that could be described as "management by walking around"—i.e., the direct overseeing of subordinates' task performance—as a method of insuring that work is performed effectively. This method may be both effective and efficient in a traditional organization, where managers can step out of their offices to see and speak to multiple subordinates in a relatively short period of time.

In a virtual context, however, managers who attempt to utilize these techniques are likely to spend a significant portion of their work day on the telephone trying to reach their subordinates. It may take longer to contact them than in traditional organizations because subordinates are dispersed, and the fact that they are not co-located may make it more difficult for the manager to be helpful and constructive even once contact is made. Furthermore, for virtual employees, having to respond to messages from their manager may be viewed as an imposition and may be perceived as a sign that their manager does not trust them to be productive when they are out of sight. Subordinates may resist or react negatively to the same managerial actions that are viewed positively in traditional work contexts. As a result, managers may find that the supervisory practices that were effective and welcomed when subordinates were in the office may take longer, be less effective, and possibly even be resented when their employees telecommute (regardless of the work location of the manager). Managers may therefore feel less effective and less respected, thus threatening their esteem.

Virtual work may even call into question the need for managers, and thus may have an acute impact on managers' perception that they are important and valued at work. Specifically, when employees spend most of their time away from the office, it is far more efficient for them to be self-organizing—i.e., assuming some of the responsibilities that would traditionally be the role of their supervisor. For example, they might become proficient at activities such as pacing themselves, motivating themselves, independently searching for feedback to assess their performance, and making decisions without relying on consultation with their managers. If employees perform these duties themselves, their managers are likely to feel that the responsibilities that determined their importance in (and their value to) the organization are diminished. As a result, managers' sense of esteem may be threatened.

The lifecycle of virtual work initiatives may present another source of negative feedback and, consequently, esteem threat. Specifically, virtual work organizations are subject to "critical mass" effects, meaning that peak efficiency and productivity are achieved only when a certain minimum participation level is reached (Garud, 1997). At the most concrete level, for example, setting up a home office for telecommuters requires some cost. The offsetting real estate cost savings that result when centralized office space is reduced can only be achieved when a certain minimum number of employees telecommute. Critical mass impacts efficiency of time as well as money: for example, managers have to progress along a steep learning curve to meet the challenges of managing from a distance. The learning process must be endured for a single telecommuting subordinate or for a whole workgroup. Thus, managers' first experiences with virtual work are likely to involve negative feedback until a critical mass is achieved, and the point of critical mass is frequently unclear, "a priori". Thus, at the start of a virtual work initiative, managers are likely to receive feedback suggesting that their attempts at managing virtual work are unsuccessful. If they attribute any of these early setbacks to themselves, their initial experience with virtual work is likely to be esteem-threatening.

Threats to Control

All individuals are concerned with maintaining a sense of control—specifically, belief in their self-efficacy and their ability to avoid discomforting uncertainty. For managers in particular, their belief that they are capable of controlling important outcomes may be an especially important self-cognition because maintaining control may be the most salient of managers' various responsibilities. This is particularly true in traditional, hierarchical and centralized organizations.

Managers' sense of control may be diminished by changes accompanying virtual work, whether those managers telecommute themselves or not. Consider, for example, the fact that managers' evaluations and career outcomes typically depend upon the performance and productivity of the work unit they supervise. Thus, managers are likely to be highly concerned with maintaining work unit performance and productivity at a high level, and changing subordinates' behaviors if their performance is projected to be lower than desired. The tools that managers typically employ to insure subordinates' performance include their power to evaluate and reward their subordinates.

In a virtual organization, however, the techniques that managers employ to evaluate performance may be inefficient or ineffective. For example, it is nearly impossible for managers to supervise their subordinates' behaviors when those employees telecommute because there is no efficient way to see or keep track of employees' actions; it is far more efficient for managers to monitor their subordinates' outcomes instead. In practice this might mean that a manager will find it more efficient to keep track of the dollar value of goods sold by their subordinates rather than the subordinates' skills and behaviors. If so, subordinates will have greater discretion over the means by which they achieve outcomes, and managers will be forced to relinquish control over subordinates' behaviors, even though those behaviors are the earliest predictor of work unit performance and, therefore, managers' own evaluations.

Managers' sense of control may also be threatened because the transition to virtual work introduces uncertainty, both real and perceived. For example, it is difficult to predict whether subordinates will adjust to telecommuting, which managerial skills or techniques will be effective, the true costs of the new way of working and the potential productivity gains or losses that may result. Furthermore, managers may be subject to a type of "second order uncertainty"—because subordinates are dispersed in a virtual context, managers may not even have access to the information that would help them determine what skills they need or what the costs and benefits of virtual work are.

Managers may be able to retain a sense of control over their work unit in a virtual context if they trust their subordinates. However, trust may need to be built up in interactions over time. A significant barrier to trust is the fact that some virtual workers will be new employees (either new to the organization or new to the work unit). As a result, they may not be socialized sufficiently to build a trusting relationship with their supervisor or their peers. In such instances, managers' perception of loss of control may be very acute.

Furthermore, the context in which many organizations implement virtual work initiatives has the effect of raising the stakes; i.e., increasing the perceived cost of failure. When telecommuting is voluntary, it is frequently up to a manager to decide whether to permit a subordinate to go virtual. As a result, that subordinate's performance in a virtual context is the responsibility of, and will be attributed to, the manager. When telecommuting is mandatory, it is often undertaken in the context of broader cost-cutting initiatives. Cost-cutting programs are often perceived as a potential threat to jobs, and in recent years middle managers have been hard-hit by layoffs (Wiesenfeld & Thibault, 1997). These threats personalize the uncertainty that managers experience. Thus, virtual work may threaten both managers' sense of control over their own personal outcomes (e.g., their career prospects), and their sense of control over organizational outcomes (e.g., their work unit productivity and their subordinates' satisfaction).

RESPONSES TO SELF-THREAT

Individuals have attitudinal and behavioral responses to self-threat. These include (a) the immediate manifestations of the experience of threat, and (b) individuals' adaptive attempts to protect or restore the self following the experience of threat. According to previous research, individuals' natural responses to the experience of self-threat include feelings of depression, anger and stress, attempts to withdraw from the threatening situation, attitudinal and behavioral rigidity, aversion to risk, and efforts to seize control (see Wiesenfeld & Thibault, 1997, for a review). These emotions and activities may be adaptive for individuals personally because they may ultimately lead to a reduction in the experience of threat or a restoration of the self-following the threat. However, if managers indulge in these emotions and behaviors, the long-term outcomes may be damaging both to the organization and to the managers personally.

Consider, for example, individuals' instinctive response to a perceived loss of control. Research suggests that individuals in such positions frequently attempt to seize control over those portions of their life that they are capable of controlling in an effort to reassure themselves about their ability to affect important outcomes (Wiesenfeld & Thibault, 1997). Imagine that the individual who experiences a threat to control is the manager of telecommuting subordinates. As indicated above, it may be most effective and efficient to allow virtual workers to be self-organizing to the extent possible, because traditional control mechanisms may be difficult and expensive to implement and resented by the workers themselves. However, a manager who feels threatened will be particularly averse to allowing self-organization among his/her subordinates. Such a manager may instead insist upon greater oversight and supervision in a vain attempt to restore a sense of control. For example, a manager who feels threatened may insist that telecommuting subordinates return to centralized office locations—a request that subordinates may resent and resist. In such cases, the more that managers attempt to seize control, the more resistance they will get from subordinates and the less effective their attempts to achieve control will be. This vicious cycle is harmful not only to the manager but also to the motivation and productivity of the entire work unit, because motivation and productivity in a virtual setting may be best achieved by allowing subordinates to self-organize.

While some managers may seize control in a "fight" response to the experience of self-threat, other managers may initiate a "flight" response. Specifically, some threatened managers may attempt to withdraw from the threatening situation either psychologically or behaviorally. This response may be an attempt by managers to shield themselves from threat by de-emphasizing the domain from which the threat comes. Although this strategy may be effective in reducing the experience of threat, it may be harmful to subordinates and possibly to the managers themselves in the long run. In particular, virtual workers tend to feel isolated and may be especially sensitive to the degree of support that they receive from other members of the organization (Raghuram, Wiesenfeld & Garud, 1996). For many teleworkers, their supervisor is the only organization member with whom they have regular contact, so they may be especially sensitive to the cues they receive from managers. If their managers are withdrawn and uninvolved, subordinates may feel neglected and abandoned. They may perceive that their career prospects within the organization are limited. Even if teleworkers welcome the freedom of diminished supervision, their reduced attachment to the organization and fellow group members may discourage their exhibition of organizational citizenship behaviors.

In sum, managers' experience of self-threat is likely to trigger responses that are potentially harmful to subordinate motivation and productivity, and in the long run may even be harmful to the managers themselves (Wiesenfeld & Thibault, 1997). If virtual work is experienced by managers as a threat to their identity, esteem, and sense of control, the self-protective responses that are triggered may limit the scope and viability of virtual work initiatives. Furthermore, if "critical mass" effects are relevant to the success of virtual work, then the early resistance of managers may prevent an organization from ever achieving the full benefit of virtual work.

IMPLICATIONS

The arguments that we have advanced have important implications for research and practice. First, the role of managers has received very little attention in research on virtual work to date. We suggest that managers play a critical role in the growth and success of virtual work initiatives.

Their efforts to promote or discourage virtual work may influence the rate at which employees choose to participate in virtual work programs, and managers' support of employees may determine whether organizations' virtual work experiments are successful.

To understand the attitudes and behaviors of managers in virtual organizations, we argue that it is important to recognize that managers may experience virtual work as a threat to the self. Changes accompanying virtual work are likely to threaten managers' identity, esteem, and sense of control. Whether managers openly acknowledge their experience of self-threat or not, virtual work initiatives may trigger a dynamic self process in which managers experience a threat to the self and respond with attempts to protect or restore the self. Many of these coping responses, such as attempts to seize control or withdraw from the situation, may have harmful implications for the motivation and productivity of managers' work units and ultimately for the organization and the managers' career.

If managers may experience self-threat as a result of virtual work, future research might examine the conditions under which such self-threat may be reduced. For example, although it may be difficult to alter the content of virtual work, research may identify ways to manage the transition process so that it is less likely to be experienced as self-threatening. For example, if managers participate in shaping the structures and systems supporting virtual work (rather than merely implementing policies determined at higher levels in the organizational hierarchy), they may feel less threatened by the changes that it creates. When virtual work programs are voluntary, managers often do play a significant role in structuring their subordinates' virtual work context. However, involving managers may also be beneficial in the context of mandatory virtual work initiatives because it may reduce managers' feelings of self-threat and their resulting resistance to change.

Managers may be less likely to feel threatened if they understand what is necessary for them to perform effectively in a virtual work context. Future research may help to identify the practices and skills that are most effective in managing virtual employees. For example, it is possible that managers may be more effective if they allow virtual subordinates to self-organize. Certain practices may enable such self-organization, such as evaluation and reward systems based on outcomes rather than behaviors, or use of consistent and explicit criteria rather than changing or implicit ones. It is possible that salespeople are the first to go virtual in many organizations because it may be easier for them to function independently and to quantify their performance. Managers may be most effective when they coach and empower subordinates, and their role may be to insure that subordinates obtain the resources necessary to remain productive. At NCR, the title "manager" has been replaced by "coach" throughout the organization in order to institutionalize this change in managerial responsibilities.

If virtual work does require different managerial techniques than traditional work modes, it is critical that organizations help managers to obtain the necessary skills. For example, managers may need to learn how to conduct meetings by telephone or utilize electronic means of communication. Companies such as Hewlett Packard and Merrill Lynch are utilizing simulations to help managers acquire such skills, but much more work is needed in developing such training programs.

Organizations must also reinforce managers who demonstrate effective managerial behaviors, which may require a change in the organizational culture. For example, organizations should not reward managers who are more autocratic, and the size of one's office or desk or the number of subordinates that one can command should not determine managerial status.

We assert that virtual work not only changes the location in which work is performed but also, it alters the very form and definition of organizations. For example, instituting virtual work may call into question the organization as a hierarchy. Moreover, we suggest that virtual work affects organization members at the most fundamental level—the level of their self-concept. In particular, changes that accompany virtual work may be experienced as a threat to identity, esteem, or sense of control, and this may be especially true for managers. Ultimately, the success of virtual work initiatives may depend upon acknowledging the fundamental changes that they necessitate in every aspect of organizational life.

REFERENCES

Ashforth, B. E. & Mael, F. (1989) Social identity theory and the organization. *Academy of Management Review*, **14**: 20–39.

DeSanctis, G. (1984) Attitudes toward telecommuting: implications for work-at-home programs. *Information & Management*, 7: 133–139.

Dutton, J. E. & Dukerich, J. M. (1991) Keeping an eye on the mirror: the role of image and identity in organizational adaptation. *Academy of Management Journal*, **34**: 517–554.

Dutton, J. E., Dukerich, J. M. & Harquail, C. V. (1994) Organizational images and member identification. *Administrative Science Quarterly*, **39**: 239–263.

Garud, R. (1997) Trust and virtual systems. *SternBusiness Magazine*, **Spring/Summer**: 32–35.

Garud, R. & Dunbar, R. (1998) *Best Practices in the Virtual Workplace.* New York: Stern School of Business, New York University.

Miles, R. & Snow, C. (1986) Organizations: new concepts for new forms. *California Management Review*, **Spring**: 62–73.

Nohria, N. & Eccles, R. G. (1992) *Networks and Organizations: Structure, Form and Action*. Boston, MA: Harvard Business School Press.

Pierce, J. L., Gardner, D. G., Cummings, L. L. & Dunham, R. B. (1989) Organization-based self-esteem: construct definition, measurement, and validation. *Academy of Management Journal*, **32**: 622–648.

Powell, W. (1990) Neither market nor hierarchy: network forms of organization. In B. Staw and L. Cummings (Eds), *Research in Organizational Behavior*, Vol. 12, pp. 295–336, Greenwich, CT: JAI Press.

Raghuram, S. (1996) Knowledge creation in the telework context. *International Journal of Technology Management*, **11**: 859–870.

Raghuram, S., Wiesenfeld, B. M., & Garud, R. (1996) *Working from a Distance*. Paper presented to the Organization and Management Theory division of the Academy of Management in Cincinnati, OH.

Shamir, B. & Salomon, I. (1985) Work at home and the quality of working life. *Academy of Management Review*, **10**: 455–464.

Turner, J. C. (1982) Toward a cognitive definition of the group. In H. Tajfel (Ed.), *Social Identity and Intergroup Relations*, pp. 123–137. Cambridge, UK: Cambridge University Press.

Wiesenfeld, B. M., Raghuram, S., & Garud, R. (1999) Communication patterns as determinants of organizational identification in a virtual organization, forthcoming in *Organization Science*, **10**: (6).

Wiesenfeld, B. M. & Thibault, V. (1997) Managers are employees, too: Exploring the relationships between procedural fairness, managers' self-perceptions, and managerial behaviors following a layoff. Academy of Management Best Papers Proceedings, pp. 359–363.

Williamson, O. E. (1991) Comparative economic organization: the analysis of discrete structural alternatives. *Administrative Science Quarterly*, **36**: 269–296.

CHAPTER 4

Human Resource Management and the Virtual Organization: Mapping the Future Research Issues

Paul R. Sparrow and Kevin Daniels
University of Sheffield, UK

INTRODUCTION

The ready availability of information networks, e-mail and portable telephones is seen as accelerating the "virtuality" of work. This reflected in radical changes in organization structure, coordination systems and task specification. Companies such as Reebok, Nike and Puma rely on the use of computer networks and small hubs of designers to coordinate the production of products and services. Dell, Gateway, Benetton and IKEA focus on core value-added processes and alliances with suppliers to respond to a rapidly changing marketplace. To understand the development towards virtuality, analysts have relied on futuristic scenarios of life in the virtual organization derived from case studies or simulation (Jarvenpaa & Ives, 1994). Although such techniques often make optimistic assumptions, they do serve to demonstrate the radical impact that new information and communication technologies can have on human resource management (HRM). Importantly, they surface the assumptions we make about employee motivation to live in a world of virtual organizations, their competence to deliver its required products and services, and their capacities to cope with its demands. The changing nature of information, organization and management forces us to reconsider how best to develop and utilize human capability and potential (Wigand, Picot & Reichwald, 1997).

Trends in Organizational Behavior, Volume 6. Edited by C. L. Cooper and D. M. Rousseau.
Copyright © 1999 John Wiley & Sons, Ltd.

Even if a liberal interpretation of "virtuality" is taken to include flat structures, a degree of ad-hocracy and team-orientation, then most organizations are moving in this direction in small evolutionary steps (Stanworth, 1998). Moreover, current analysis tends to confound separate levels of analysis and there is little hard empirical evidence on the impacts of virtual organization on behavior. Our understanding of the implications of working in the virtual organization is being built by analyzing some of the main ingredients. There is a danger in this, in that as any cook knows, the final blend has a character all of its own, above and beyond the constituent ingredients.

In this Chapter, we focus on the trends associated with the most documented HRM issues that will accompany virtual organizations. Strategic areas of organizational behavior can best be understood by studying the phenomenon across levels of analysis (Schuler, 1997). In order to elicit the issues, we focus on *three* streams of literature, each of which constitutes a separate level of analysis, and tackles different phenomena:

(1) *Organizational* level—issues of organizational form, work organization and organizational learning associated with the virtual organization, the demise of hierarchy and the electronic office (Stanworth, 1998).
(2) *Workforce* level—innovative ways of working such as teleworking, telecommuting, and the boundaryless organization (Stanworth, 1998).
(3) *Individual* level—key organizational behaviors that come to the fore in a teleworking environment, such as: the information search, conceptual flexibility and problem solving competencies needed (Wigand, Picot & Reichwald, 1997); job design and jobs-based flexibility implications (Sparrow, 1998a); problems of information overload (Sparrow, 1998b) or techno-stress associated with multi-tasking; and changes in levels of well-being (Daniels, 1999).

WHAT BECOMES VIRTUAL AND WITH WHAT IMPACT ON ORGANIZATIONAL BEHAVIOR?

At the organizational level of analysis the virtual organization is a loose web of individuals, capital and technologies which may operate in amalgamation as a flexible organizational form. It involves project-focused, collaborative networks uninhibited by time and space. Driven by the necessities of globalization and knowledge-based competition, it is staffed by knowledge workers (with specialist knowledge, relevant professional expertise, and enterprising and innovative qualities) brought together under short term market relationships. It operates without apparent structure (the removal of traditional hierarchies does not remove structure in terms of power and resource control), has ever-changing boundaries, and dissolves as soon as a project is completed. It contains a number of paradoxes. It stands in contrast to many tenets of resource-based theory. It is hard to see how it can help firms develop and leverage "core competencies" when they rent all their human capital. It is also hard to create resources that cannot be imitated when the knowledge-based resources are highly mobile project participants. There are also difficulties in seeing how tacit knowledge and knowledge transfer unfolds without a stable cadre of core managers. For a virtual organization to be a preferable option to other organizational forms, it has to emphasize (Stanworth, 1998; Wigand, Picot & Reichwald, 1997):

(1) Employment that terminates with the completion of project responsibilities. No obligation to employ social actors under permanent or exclusive contracts and no unmanageable costs in not doing so (e.g., withdrawal behaviors associated with breach of the psychological contract).
(2) Bringing together heterogeneous competencies, each with differentiated performance profiles, but that require a symbiotic, interdependent, relationship and configuration in order to realize performance goals.
(3) Modular work, i.e., fundamental fragments that are best conducted with a decentralized decision making competence.
(4) Time and spatial distribution, i.e., choice over the location and temporal boundaries that may be used to divide the labor process.
(5) Operation within a context of an uncertain and volatile market (short life-cycle products, unstable sales, high number of competitors, high cost resources and high labor competition).
(6) No claim to the governance of future projects.

It is clear that the virtual organization will have limited application. The dangers inherent in generalized analyses of the implications of such virtual organization can be seen in the various definitions and taxonomies used to classify activity at the workforce level. Teleworkers work at a place other than where the results of the work need to be used (Bertin & Denbigh, 1996), supported by information and telecommunications technologies (Gray, Hodson & Gordon, 1993). The attention given to teleworking often conjures up images of restricted choice in job design, including: disembodied employees working from home in isolation and on a piecework basis; or boring, routine and deadening jobs akin to the single function information technology (IT) roles that first emerged, such as word processing and code writers (Tapscott, 1996). In practice, the *contractual status* of teleworkers—indeed all workers in a virtual organization—tends to fall into one of two categories:

(1) Workers on flexible employment contracts, with portfolios of work across a variety of jobs, operating as enterprising free agents on a self-employed status (Negroponte, 1995), i.e., hollow organizations that are little more than a collection of commercial contracts.
(2) Privileged core employees, enjoying high trust relationships, and given autonomy over work location and time (Handy, 1995), i.e., the re-emergence of industrial guilds serviced by a small technical and commercial elite.

Moreover, three distinct *forms* of teleworking are typically identified (Andriessen, 1991; Gray, Hodson & Gordon, 1993; Huws, 1994): home-based telework, where workers do their job at home; mobile telework, where workers spend a lot of time travelling and/or on customers' premises; and telework at remote offices, known variously as "satellite offices", "telecentres" or "telecottages". If the formal contract and terms of employment vary, so must the psychological contract and resultant behaviors associated with trust, commitment, socialization, and motivation. By concentrating merely on the location and technical set up, any analysis of the virtual organization misses many complexities. There is nothing inherent in the technology associated with the virtual organization that will necessarily result in improvements in the quality of working life (Tapscott, 1996). A more contextual approach is needed. Lamond, Daniels and Standen (1997) conceptualize telework as a bundle of practices varying across five dimensions:

(1) *IT usage*—extent of use of telecommunications/IT links (home/mobile computer, fax, modem, phone, mobile phone, use of WWW sites).
(2) *Knowledge intensity*—extent of knowledge required, ease of output measures and autonomy of work.
(3) *Intra-organizational contact*—extent of contact with other organizational members.
(4) *Extra-organizational contact*—extent of contact with other people from beyond organizational boundaries.
(5) *Location*—time spent in different locations: traditional office, home, remote office/telecottage, nomadic.

This dimensional approach emphasizes that there can be no "one-size-fits-all" approach to HRM in the virtual organization. It reflects the early dimensional approach to structure adopted by the Aston researchers in the 1970s. If organizational forms are classified as high/low across these five dimensions, this suggests 32 types of virtual organization. Positioning hypothetical types in this way may clarify when the virtual organization should be a "stand alone" development or when in practice it should be an adjunct to a more traditional form of organization. Figure 4.1 both maps out the future HRM research issues that must be examined in the light of such contingencies, and acts as a guide to the content and structure of this chapter.

Moreover, there are differences between allowing certain levels of telework, and designing a successful virtual organization. We are tempted through popular image to see virtual organizations as loose connections of highly proficient professionals who can be left to "do their own thing" and relied on to produce world beating products or services. If virtual organization becomes an established organizational form, we will see analyses of "the failed virtual organization". Currently many seem to see the virtual organization as little more than an administrative convenience—a temporary attractor of self-organizing actors. If we are to avoid the creation of "convenience virtuality", whereby managers and organizations simply drift towards the concept by allowing certain people tasks units to become managed at a distance for some of their time on an *ad hoc* basis, or by being driven solely by the technical elements of the system or labor market of one or two in-dividuals, then we will need to see much more strategic thought amongst the organization design community. Should this happen, we should expect to see the old socio-technical systems thinking replaced by more detailed consideration of jobs-based flexibility. Organization behavior theorists will have to advise on the simultaneous manipulation of four elements (Sparrow, 1998b) whilst ensuring that the recommended solutions are consistent with the knowns and givens of human nature and interests:

(1) The various components that are best bundled together into definable "jobs" or roles in the virtual organization (through the tasks, operations, work elements and duties that are deemed still necessary).
(2) Redesign of the context into which these jobs or roles are placed and the position of the virtual job in the broader organization design (through the family of jobs to which the role holder is deemed to belong, their perceived occupation, the career stream to which the requisite skills belong, and the work process of which it forms a part).
(3) The way in which virtual jobs relate to and interact with each other (through the roles assigned to jobs, the information and control systems, the relative levels of power they possess).

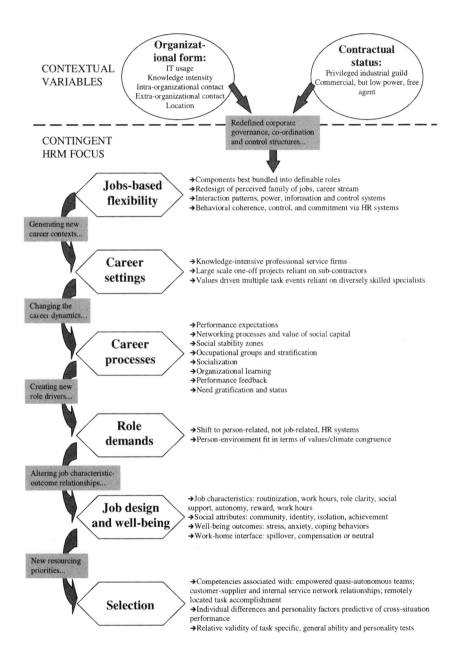

Figure 4.1   HRM issues triggered by virtual organization

(4) The way in which HRM systems integrate the new bundles of virtual jobs into the strategic process or purpose of the organization (through the way in which member contributions to their virtual roles are coordinated, controlled and committed to).

VIRTUAL ORGANIZATION AND CAREER DYNAMICS

The rise of project-based careers and the creation of temporary organizations for project-based work go hand-in-hand. Therefore we need to consider work on career behavior in a variety of settings that contain elements of virtual organization. This may either illuminate new patterns of behavior, or show how known elements in the human repertoire will be adapted to new realities. Proxy settings to explore include:

(1) Knowledge-intensive professional service firms, such as law, management consulting, architecture and advertising.
(2) Sectors that manage large scale, one-off projects that have a high reliance on subcontractors, such as the film, construction, oil exploration and semiconductor industries.
(3) Rapid response, values-driven, multiple task work that combines and recombines diversely-skilled people, such as non-governmental organizations, aid agencies and charities.

De Fillippi and Arthur's (1998) analysis of project-based careers in the film making industry serves as a useful prototype for some facets of the virtual organization. They analyzed how career processes influence, and are influenced by, successive project-based enterprise activities. Using qualitative research methods of 16 participants during the middle weeks of the production of a US–UK feature film, they examined the team's reasons for involvement, previous social relationships with other team members, interdependencies between tasks, innovative work elements, and expected impacts on careers. From an organizational behavior perspective issues of loyalty, commitment, socialization and trust become paramount. In a virtual organization, corporate governance rules become critical in managing variable employment numbers. The number of team members may grow exponentially within a few weeks, and then fall off within a similar period. Physical assets, such as office space, are generally also temporary and out-sourced. The strategic vision of the enterprise is often inherited by participants, rather than communicated through the traditional recipe of mission statements and objective-based performance management and appraisal systems. It has to be in place before the enterprise is formed, but is shared in an evolving fashion with an ever-widening network of virtual organization actors and support staff. We can draw the following lessons about life in the virtual organization from De Fillippi and Arthur's (1998) analysis:

(1) Recruitment is conducted under time-pressure and carries high performance expectations. Requisite abilities must be signalled and revolve around experience and track record.
(2) However, human capital (each knowing one's trade) and social capital (each knowing one another) become inextricably linked. Inter-project employment is highly dependent on the career competencies of participants. Network processes and skills become critical and reputation is a key asset. Reputation and knowledge are owned and managed by, and distributed across, a loose network of project participants (Hedlund, 1994). Knowledge management is driven by personal and reputational relationships, whilst recruitment becomes dependent on the judgements made by trusted principal lieutenants, who in turn fill out the crew. In practice, everyone comes with a team, because most key roles are too big for any one person. Socially interconnected networks can soon become apparent over time.
(3) The formation of some stability in social relationships is not an automatic prerequisite of success. Moderate levels of experience of working together are helpful, but too much prior experience is harmful and can be replaced by good corporate governance and team management techniques (Argote, 1993).
(4) Work pace is variable. Given the higher interdependence on other members, certainty over exact timings is impossible. The need for a state of readiness to be mobilized at a moment's notice is high.
(5) Not all virtual team members are high skill–high reputation individuals. They are stratified into three occupational groups determined by career development processes: principals (those behind the strategy formation and virtual team concept), professionals (hired to form the organization and apply particular knowledge-based competence) and apprentices (joining the enterprise to perform mundane but necessary tasks). Apprentices, or runners, become exposed to the chaotic interconnections among specialized staff. Their behavior is incidental to the current project, but indicative of commitment and compatibility for forthcoming projects.
(6) The value of idleness is characterized by learning by watching others during one's own downtime. Master–apprentice relationships and craft-based learning techniques become important in virtual organizations and form the basis of socialization into shared values and tacit knowledge. This learning is particular to their role and the unfolding of their careers.

(7) Organizational learning does not reside in the standard operating procedures, systems and structures. It resides in a process of episodic learning and the creation of a collective memory of what works and what does not, shared across project participants (Bird, 1996). Retention and protection of information within the organization becomes problematic.

(8) Job/project feedback and legitimized status is very short term. Virtual organizations often require a heavy front-end investment to create the systems and staffing structures. Awareness of the precarious nature of a project, preferences of investors and issues of cost control are uppermost in the minds of most team members. Long term feedback (of the film success) and revenue generation often follow once the virtual organization has been disbanded, with the symbolic departure of key actors and destruction of the team before any critical review. Gratification of any need for achievement is delayed and is a secondary experience.

ROLE DEMANDS AND DRIVERS

We should expect the virtual organization to have an impact on a wide range of occupational behavior. Attention to the role demands that subsequently drive resourcing decisions such as recruitment has found attention in discussion of the "boundaryless organization" i.e. where the limitations inherent in separating people, tasks, processes and places are replaced by an emphasis on moving ideas, information, decisions, talent and action to where they are most needed (Ashkenas et al., 1995). The relevance of some job analysis and recruitment techniques has been questioned in this context (Nelson, 1997). Traditional selection techniques rely on matching the skills and knowledge of the person with the demands and requirements of the job. As organizations reallocate knowledge, information, power and rewards in a virtual organization, the current focus in the HRM literature on person- as opposed to job-related performance management systems will become central. It will not be possible to accurately price the evolving set of tasks and activities built into internal roles in the labor market. Jobs in the virtual organization will not have value, only the people. This will force organizational psychologists to abandon much of the job–person fit paradigm that underlies their work on selection and assessment (Herriot and Anderson, 1997). Researchers will still be analyzing person–environment fit, but using different criteria for each element. On the person side the shift is towards a different set of competencies and personality factors, whilst on the environment side, the shift is towards organizational values/climate fit and broad role analysis.

JOB DESIGN AND WELL-BEING

In the area of job design and well-being in the virtual organization especially there has been a great deal of speculation, but very little evidence (Qvortrup, 1998). The need to consider job design issues and the resultant work–life balance is clear. The shift towards virtual organization is associated with a fundamental re-alignment and re-ordering of jobs. It impacts both the content of jobs and the way in which they relate to each other (through the roles assigned to jobs, the information and control systems, the relative levels of power they possess) (Sparrow, 1998a). It makes it possible to work all the time.

Knowledge-based jobs are assumed to require greater skills, have greater variety and offer more potential for a high quality of working life (QWL) (Tapscott, 1996). The premise that Tayloristic solutions are inappropriate for work in the virtual organization rests on *three* main arguments:

(1) Modern information systems are shifting to systems built around multi-function workstations that integrate data, text, voice, image and (soon) video media. This makes it both easier, indeed unavoidable, to design "whole" jobs.
(2) The element of risk and trust implicit in virtual relationships and modern organizational forms necessitates an emphasis on high commitment relationships, which in turn are best engendered by high performance HRM systems.
(3) Teleworking practices associated with virtual organizations are characterized by a number of job characteristics linked to psychological well-being.

The negative job characteristics involved in teleworking that have been linked to psychological well-being are: increased routinization; longer hours and increases in perceived work demands; decreased role clarity as information degrades through telecommunications; poorer physical working conditions; less social support from work; poorer social position; and fewer career opportunities (Olsen, 1985, Gurstein, 1991, Gray, Hodson & Gordon, 1993, Haddon & Lewis, 1994, Huws, 1994, Gillespie, Richardson & Cornford, 1995, Tucknutt, Griggs & Maternaghan, 1995). On the positive side there is greater job autonomy and more money (in the short term) because of reduced commuting, lunches and clothing costs, and a shift to above-market pay rates to compensate for the added degree of risk and insecurity (Kraut, 1987, Gurstein, 1991, Gray, Hodson & Gordon, 1993, Haddon & Lewis, 1994, Gillespie, Richardson & Cornford, 1995, Mirchandani, 1998). However, the majority of this evidence refers to home-based teleworking, and is based usually on small scale qualitative studies without comparisons with traditional office-based workers doing similar jobs. For example, in a study of 62 homeworkers Baruch and Nicholson (1997) found that the experience generally led to: an increase in working hours; a perceived increase in performance; less work-related stress but more home-related stress; and changed social relationships, as barriers between the home–work interface dissolve. There were wide individual differences in the ability and desire to adapt to homeworking.

A recent comparative study found no relationship between work-related psychological well-being and the extent of home-based teleworking or mobile teleworking (Daniels, 1999). Neither were there differences in well-being for home-based teleworkers across a range of job characteristics. The job characteristics of home-based teleworkers may not differ greatly from those of their office-based counterparts, or alternatively home-based teleworkers may take steps to eliminate negative job features inherent in home-based work—such as social isolation—by engaging in non-paid activities to compensate. In this study, however, there were differences in job characteristics between traditional office workers and mobile teleworkers. Mobile teleworkers reported greater job demands. Less frequent, mobile teleworkers reported more role conflict than both traditional office workers and frequent mobile teleworkers. For the most frequent mobile teleworkers, increased job demands were compensated for by greater autonomy, participation in decisions, work variety, role clarity and career opportunities. For less frequent mobile teleworkers, job demands and greater role conflict were not off-set by positive job features. They reported greater negative influences of work on their non-work life. There was also a relationship between home-based teleworking and the negative impact of work on non-work life, moderated by work-related anxiety. The negative impact of work on non-work life was greatest for anxious home-based teleworkers. Anxiety directs attention towards the threatening aspects of the environment (Williams *et al.*, 1996). For traditional office workers, the home environment does not present any anxiety-provoking work cues, but for home-based teleworkers they remain. The permeability of the home–work interface, thought to be generally greater for home-based teleworkers (Ahrentzen, 1990), appears to be dependent upon levels of anxiety.

Future research into job design and well-being in virtual organizations needs to build upon comparative studies—preferably through longitudinal and quasi-experimental designs. Evidence from a wider variety of samples is needed, but a number of questions also need to be addressed. These include: the influence of the home environment on work related well-being and how people cope, compensate for or accommodate stressors in one life domain in other domain (Lambert, 1990); the

influence of working from satellite offices or telecottages on job characteristics and well-being; and the joint effects of changes in organizational
forms, ways of working and changes in employment contracts upon well-
being. We also need to disentangle findings that may be based on the
experience of "enthusiastic early adopters" (with a positive frame of
mind driven by the potential that the virtual organization offers for autonomy, independence, responsibility for developing and customizing their
knowledge base, and opportunity for increased earnings through competition for their services) and reluctant (later) adopters who have less
control over their destiny (who mourn what they perceive as lost values
at work such as a sense of community, shared goals and the pride and
identity associated with group achievement). Researchers will need to
identify the most effective "functional equivalents" for those job characteristics that are perceived as being lost. They will need to re-explore the
links between individual differences, perceived satisfaction with the job
characteristics implicit in the virtual organization and how people cope
with the changing and ambiguous boundaries between work and non-
work life inherent in virtual work.

SELECTION IN THE VIRTUAL ORGANIZATION

We can expect to see the following three trends in related selection
research:

(1) The examination of competencies and behaviors associated with
    proxy forms of work organization.
(2) Selecting for person–organization fit in terms of values or organiza-
    tional climate.
(3) Seeking personality and aptitude traits associated with effective per-
    formance in a variety of contexts.

It may be better to select people on their ability to develop their skills,
and their ability to motivate themselves. In delineating employee competencies associated with effective performance in the virtual organization,
the resultant characteristics reflect strongly those identified for: em-
powered, quasi-autonomous self-managing teams (with responsibility for
the quality of task accomplishment, setting goals, self-control, and decentralized decision making, problem solution and conflict management)
(Katzenbach & Smith, 1994; Manz & Sims, 1993); behaviors demonstrated
by employees working in network relationships across customer–
supplier and internal service interfaces (Johansen & Swigart, 1994); and
characteristics associated with remotely located task accomplishment

(Godehart, 1994; Glaser & Glaser, 1995). The key challenges for selection systems involve conceptualizing performance beyond the narrow focus often used in validation studies. Performance should be viewed as consisting of individual performance, the wider contribution to team performance through extra-role behavior, adaptability to new and changing forms of work organization, and the ability to acquire knowledge and motivation. This may enable researchers to establish a more inclusive set of correlates of performance in terms of personality traits and person–organization fit.

When asked about the qualities most inducive to teleworking, existing teleworkers highlight self motivation, tenacity, organizational skills, self-confidence, time management skills, computer literacy and integrity (*Management Today*, 1998). This is a similar set of competencies to those identified by the writers above, who add good subject-matter knowledge. Those responsible for managing and leading the virtual team will additionally need to demonstrate leadership that generates organizational learning, political capabilities, and the capacity for trust building (Wigand, Picot & Reichwald, 1997). Many of these attributes are intangible when it comes to assessment, and most certainly have not been validated by traditional research methods.

Another approach is to select people whose values are already consonant with the organization's culture (*cf*. Bowen, Ledford & Nathan, 1991). Evidence indicates that where there is a close fit between an employee's values and the organizational culture, then there is a greater chance that the employee will be satisfied with his/her job and committed to the organization (O'Reilly, Chatman & Caldwell, 1991). In virtual organizations, selecting to maximize person–organization fit may be especially important: there are fewer opportunities to socialize employees where organizations are short lived and dispersed over large geographic areas, and the culture itself may be less pronounced. In such circumstances basic value fit becomes important.

A third approach emphasizes the personality traits linked consistently, across contexts, to performance. Of the major individual differences, Behling (1998) argues that general intelligence and conscientiousness are the most important in predicting job performance where employees are required to develop their skills on the job, to engage in a high degree of problem solving, to adapt rapidly to changes and have a great deal of autonomy. Not surprisingly, Behling considers general intelligence the main driver of successful problem solving, skill and knowledge acquisition and adaptability to changes. Conscientious employees are thought to be more trustworthy and motivated when not supervised directly, and are also likely to get more out of training programs. A contingency approach might be more suitable for other major individual differences.

Home-based telework characterized by low intra- or extra-organizational communication might be more suitable for introverts, but mobile telework characterized by high degrees of extra-organizational communication might be more suitable for extroverts and people who score high on measures of openness to experience (cf. Lamond, Daniels & Standen, 1997). Currently the order of success in predicting work and occupational performance ranges from task specific tests (most predictive), general ability tests to personality tests (less predictive). The relative order of validity may change as evidence emerges from virtual organizations.

CONCLUSION

The shift towards virtual organization triggers two ongoing debates within the HRM field: the relevance of traditional forms of HRM to future organizational forms; and the shift from person–job fit to person–role or person–values fit as the guiding paradigm for resourcing decisions. It could be argued that we have taken too traditional a perspective in this Chapter, by assuming that many aspects of organization (such as power and resource control hierarchies) remain, as will the core HRM concerns that we discuss. Relating this discussion to the contemporary strategic HRM debate, is a radical change in store? Will virtual organizations become self-selecting groups of entrepreneurs, where everybody becomes their own HRM manager? Who will care about well-being, career dynamics and person–organization fit? Should we just focus attention on the organizational behavior and people-management issues associated with small and medium enterprises and loose networks of entrepreneurs? Such radical shifts in the agenda must of course be signalled as a possible end-point, but to the extent that researchers believe that for the foreseeable future shifts towards virtuality are best seen in the context of the following three developments, traditional HRM concerns will still form the major part of the agenda:

(1) Shifts within the employees' portfolio of work experiences, limited to episodes within their career or their working year, and buttressed by spells of more formal employment and organizational attachment.
(2) Organizational experiments confined to special projects staffed by small cadres of professional project managers.
(3) A small, but growing, number of new business start-up ventures established in the entrepreneurial spirit.

This suggests that we will see the development of a specialized field of study, akin to the study of expatriates or international managers, which is still anchored by HRM considerations associated with the interface of such managers with the greater, more stable, organizational form that spawned them.

However, it is clear that research and practice in the area of virtual organizations face a number of challenges. To establish the most suitable HRM content for each context, researchers need to examine a number of assumptions with rigorous empirical methodology. Whilst research should seek to build cumulatively on traditional quantitative approaches—such as surveys and quasi-experimental intervention studies—researchers should be aware of two issues. First, theory in this area is nascent. Second, locating and sampling workers from virtual organizations is difficult—because of their ephemeral nature. Both these factors mean that *theory building* research—involving, for example, ethnography and action research—is as valuable, if not more so, as testing predictions in virtual organizations from extant organizational behavior theory. In particular, research that investigates the knowledge and cognition of virtual organizational members may shed crucial light on the experience of virtual work, and the relation of HRM practices to the experience of virtual work. A pluralistic research approach is needed in this area, to stretch the limits of theory developed from research in traditional organizations, and to provide new theoretical insights. Creating a clear conceptualization and taxonomy of virtual organizations, and supporting work practices such as telework, should help further the development of new theory or the modification of existing theory.

ACKNOWLEDGEMENT

We would like to thank David Buchanan, Peter Herriot, David Lamond, Nigel Nicholson, Roy Payne, Randall Schuler, Toby Wall and Mike West for their comments on an earlier draft of this chapter.

REFERENCES

Ahrentzen, S. B. (1990)   Managing conflict by managing boundaries: how professional home workers cope with multiple roles at home. *Environment and Behavior*, **22**: 723–752.

Andriessen, J. H. E. (1991)   Mediated communication and new organizational forms. In C. L. Cooper & I. T. Robertson (Eds), *International Review of Industrial and Organizational Psychology*. Chichester: Wiley.

Argote, L. (1993)   Group and organizational learning curves: individual, system and environmental components, *British Journal of Social Psychology*, **32**: 31–51.

Ashkensas, R., Ulrich, D., Jick, T. & Kerr, S. (1995)   *The Boundaryless Organization: Breaking the Chains of Organizational Structure*. San Francisco: Jossey-Bass.

Baruch, Y. and Nicholson, N. (1997)   Home, sweet work: requirements for effective home working, *Journal of General Management*, 23(2): 15–30.

Behling, O. (1998)   Employee selection: will intelligence and conscientiousness do the job? *Academy of Management Executive*, 12(1): 77–86.

Bertin, I., Denbigh, A. (1996)   *The Teleworking Handbook: New Ways of Working in the Information Society*. London: The Telecottage Association.

Bird, A. (1996)   Careers as repositories of knowledge: considerations for boundaryless careers. In M. B. Arthur & D. M. Rousseau (Eds) *The Boundaryless Career*. New York: Oxford University Press.

Bowen, D. E., Ledford Jr, G. E., & Nathan, B. R. (1991)   Hiring for the organization, not the job. *Academy of Management Executive*, 5: 35–50.

Daniels, K. (1999)   Home based teleworking and mobile teleworking: a study of job characteristics, well being and negative carry-over. *Work Science Report Series*, 13/14: 1535–1536. Tokyo: Institute of Science of Labour.

DeFillippi, R. J. & Arthur, M. B. (1998)   Paradox in project-based enterprise: the case of film making, *California Management Review*, 40(2): 125–139.

Glaser, W. R. & Glaser, M. O. (1995)   *Telearbeit in der Praxis*. Neuwied, Germany: Luchterhand.

Gillespie, A. E., Richardson, R. & Cornford, J. (1995)   *Review of Teleworking in Britain: Implications for Public Policy*. Report to the Parliamentary Office of Science and Technology.

Godehardt, B. (1994)   *Telearbeit: Rahmenbedingungen und Potentiale*. Opladen, Germany: Westdeutscher Verlag.

Gray, M., Hodson, N. & Gordon, G. (1993)   *Teleworking Explained*. Chichester: Wiley.

Gurstein, P. (1991). Working at home and living at home: emerging scenarios. *Journal of Architectural and Planning Research*, 8: 164–180.

Haddon, L. & Lewis, A. (1994)   The experience of teleworking: an annotated review. *The International Journal of Human Resource Management*, 5: 193–223.

Handy, C. (1995) Trust and the virtual organization, *Harvard Business Review*, 73(3): 40–50.

Hedlund, G. (1994) A model of knowledge management and the N-form corporation, *Strategic Management Journal*, 15: 73–90.

Herriot, P. & Anderson, N. (1997) Selecting for change: how will personnel and selection psychology survive? In N. Anderson and P. Herriot (Eds) *International Handbook of Selection and Assessment*. Chichester: Wiley.

Huws, U. (1994)   *Teleworking*. Brussels: European Commission's Employment Task Force (Directorate General V).

Jarvenpaa, S. L. and Ives, B. (1994)   The global network organization of the future: information management opportunities and challenges, *Journal of Management Information Systems*, 4: 25–57.

Johansen, R. & Swigart, R. (1994) *Upsizing the Individual in the Downsized Organization: Managing in the Wake of Re-engineering, Globalization, and Overwhelming Technological Change*. Reading, Mass.: Addison-Wesley.

Katzenbach, J. R. & Smith, D. K. (1994)   *The wisdom of teams*, New York: Harper Business.

Knights, D. & McCabe, D. (1998)   What happens when the phone goes wild?: staff, stress and spaces for escape in a BPR telephone banking work regime. *Journal of Management Studies*, 35: 163–194.

Kraut, R. E. (1987)   Predicting the use of technology: the case of telework. In R.E. Kraut (Ed.), *Technology and the Transformation of White-Collar Work*. Chichester: Wiley.

Lambert, S. J. (1990) Processes linking work and family: a critical review and research agenda. *Human Relations,* **43**: 239–257.

Lamond, D., Daniels, K. & Standen, P. (1997) Virtual working or working virtually? An overview of the contextual and behavioural issues in teleworking. Proceedings of the 4th International Meeting of the Decision Sciences Institute, Sydney, Australia, July.

Management Today (1998) The changing perception of teleworking: time for teleworking. *HR Strategies Update,* **April**: 16–19.

Manz, C. C. & Sims, H. P. (1993) *Business Without Bosses: How Self-managing Teams are Building High Performing Companies.* New York: Wiley.

Mirchandani, K. (1998) No longer a struggle? Teleworkers' reconstruction of the work–non-work boundary. In P. J. Jackson & J. M. Van der Wielen (Eds), *Teleworking: International Perspectives, From Telcommuting to the Virtual Organization.* London: Routledge.

Negroponte, N. (1995) *Being Digital,* London: Hodder and Stoughton.

Nelson, J. B. (1997) The boundaryless organization: implications for job analysis, recruitment and selection. *Human Resource Planning,* **20**(4): 39–49.

O'Reilly III, C. A., Chatman, J. & Caldwell, D. F. (1991) People and organizational culture: a profile comparison approach to assessing person–organization fit. *Academy of Management Journal,* **34**: 487–516.

Olsen, M. (1985) *Office Work Stations in the Home.* Washington DC: National Academy Press.

Qvortrup, L. (1998) From teleworking to networking: definitions and trends. In P. J. Jackson & J. M. Van der Wielen (Eds), *Teleworking: International Perspectives, From Telcommuting to the Virtual Organization.* London: Routledge.

Schuler, R. (1997) A strategic perspective for organizational behavior. In S. E. Jackson and C. L. Cooper (Eds) *Organizational Behavior Handbook.* New York: Wiley.

Senge, P. M. (1990) The leader's new work: building learning organizations, *Sloan Management Review,* **1**: 7–23.

Sparrow, P. R. (1998a) The pursuit of multiple and parallel organizational flexibilities: reconstituting jobs, *European Journal of Work and Organizational Psychology,* **7**(1): 79–95.

Sparrow, P. R. (1998b) Information overload. In C. Clegg, K. Legge and S. Walsh (Eds) *The Experience of Managing: A Skills Workbook.* London: Macmillan

Stanworth, C. (1998) Telework and the information age. *New Technology, Work and Employment,* **13**: 51–62.

Tapscott, D. (1996) *The Digital Economy: Promise and Peril in the Age of Networked Intelligence.* New York: McGraw-Hill.

Tucknutt, D., Griggs, J. & Maternaghan, M. (1995) *Teleworking Trial.* Ipswich: BT Laboratories, Martlesham Heath.

Wigand, R., Picot, A. & Reichwald, R. (1997) *Information, Organization and Management: Expanding Markets and Corporate Boundaries.* Chichester: Wiley.

Williams, J. M. G., Watts, F. N., MacLeod, C. & Mathews, A. (1996) *Cognitive Psychology and Emotional Disorders,* 2nd edn. Chichester: Wiley.

CHAPTER 5

The Contexts for Geographically Dispersed Teams and Networks

Susan Albers Mohrman
Marshall School of Business, University of Southern California, USA

INTRODUCTION

In this era of global integration, electronic connectivity, and network and partner structures, work is with increasing frequency performed and integrated by geographically dispersed, or distributed, teams and networks. These are groups of individuals in different locations and often in different business units or companies who share accountability for a product, service, or collective function or task, and who are interdependent in carrying out their accountabilities and thus must work collaboratively to accomplish them. A primary characteristic of these distributed structures is that, although periodic face-to-face interactions may occur from time to time, the largest part of the work is done while members are geographically separated. Consequently, face-to-face interaction must be replaced and/or supplemented with considerable coordination and integration using information technologies.

A growing literature has examined the impact of and the factors facilitating and impeding successful collaboration using various information technologies in geographically dispersed teams both within and across organizational boundaries (e.g., Johansen, 1988; Galegher, Kraut & Egido, 1990, Huber, 1990; Jarvenpaa & Ives, 1994; King, *et al.*, 1998). Much of this work focuses on benefits and costs to individuals and companies of use of such technologies, the process gains and losses of using them, and on what work is best performed electronically as opposed to face-to-face.

Trends in Organizational Behavior, Volume 6. Edited by C. L. Cooper and D. M. Rousseau.
Copyright © 1999 John Wiley & Sons, Ltd.

This Chapter examines the organizational contexts that affect distributed work: contextual features that impede or facilitate such work and the nature of the contexts that have to be built for successful functioning of distributed work structures. It builds on observations from two longitudinal, multiple company studies: one of cross-functional knowledge work teams and other lateral structures carrying out knowledge work (Mohrman, Cohen & Mohrman, 1995), and the other of the processes of transition to new lateral structures (Tenkasi, Mohrman & Mohrman, 1998). Neither of these studies focused explicitly on distributed teams; however, a number of the units we studied were geographically dispersed, and certain dynamics were evident.

After reviewing the multiple purposes and kinds of geographically dispersed teams and networks that are becoming common, I make the argument that the greater reliance on lateral structures has fundamentally changed the logic of organizing away from a primarily vertical, bureaucratic orientation, and that accommodating a new lateral logic requires rebuilding the organizational context in which work is done. This is particularly true for geographically dispersed teams. Along with geographical dispersion come often a whole host of other features such as members with varying organizational membership and with different and perhaps conflicting organizational cultures and priorities that have to be addressed in order for effective collaboration to occur. I further argue that rebuilding the new organizational contexts for distributed teams will alter behavioral dynamics in organizations significantly.

GEOGRAPHICALLY DISPERSED WORK STRUCTURES AND THEIR CONTEXTS: THE CHALLENGES OF COLLABORATION ACROSS DISTANCES

Most companies readily admit that achieving success in these structures is difficult. Working in geographically dispersed structures represents a fundamental change from the old world where people largely worked in functional groupings and sat side by side with others that they worked with in their department. Work that was done in one place was sent to others for sequential handling, or all aspects of work were done redundantly in many different, self-contained locations. Face-to-face interaction was the primary mode of coordination.

Although enabled by rapid advances in information technology, distributed work structures arise because of business need. Distributed teams and networks are becoming more frequent in large part because of two concurrent requirements for success in today's global competitive environment. Many organizations are locating operations throughout the world in order to be close to needed resources, responsive to local customers, and to gain access to world markets. At the same time, organizations are having to leverage knowledge, products and activities across their organization around the world in order to be competitive, requiring new activities to integrate across their operations. Distributed work structures arise as a result of the forces both for dispersion and integration; but it is the need to coordinate and also to take advantage of widely dispersed resources and activities that results in the current rapid increase in the application of globally dispersed teams.

The words team and network have been used in varying ways in the literature. For the purpose of this Chapter I use the word "team" to refer to an interdependent group of people collectively accountable for delivering a product or service. Networks are composed of people who are involved in dispersed activities and who perform required integration or coordination functions. Distributed teams and networks assume many forms and are established for many purposes. Some may carry out the core work of the organization. Ford Motor Co., for example, designs and manufacturers cars using "teams" of several thousand people working on multiple projects, each of which is made up of contributors spread around the globe (Ferranti, 1997). Consumer products companies often have distributed "logistics" or "product integration" networks that exist primarily to coordinate activities to ensure that the product gets to a wide range of markets in a timely, cost-effective manner. Distributed "supply chain" teams examine all the stages in the value chain from raw materials to customers and across all geographies to determine how best to make money: which products will achieve the largest pay-back; which components should be bought or made; which factories should manufacture various products; and which markets should receive priority.

Organizations also use geographically dispersed teams to improve the capabilities of the organization. Process improvement teams often consist of members from various geographical regions who collaborate to introduce new technologies and redefine core organizational processes. A large chemical company that we studied, for example, had a globally dispersed team developing a global recruitment and development system. In addition, organizations are using distributed structures for learning in order to leverage knowledge capabilities. British Petroleum's virtual knowledge sharing networks have been widely cited (e.g., Davenport & Prusak, 1998) because of their effective use of information technology to interact and to spread knowledge across the corporation.

Whether geographically dispersed or not, teams and networks are lateral structures created so that work previously done through a vertical breakdown structure is now performed laterally through structures that cut across the organization. In the traditional, bureaucratic structure tasks are analytically broken apart into various "silos" and then hierarchically into jobs and assignments that are performed by individual contributors and managed by levels of management in the silo. In lateral structures, both the performance and coordination or management of tasks are performed laterally in units consisting of the necessary contributors. One purpose for creating such lateral structures is to avoid the process losses inherent in having to deal with issues hierarchically, because authority lies above the level of those doing the work and because decision responsibility for the various aspects of a project or product is scattered across various silos.

Most geographically dispersed teams and networks perform knowledge work, work that requires the generation, compilation and interpretation of information and knowledge. Companies comprise teams by pulling expertise from wherever in the company it happens to exist. Research has found the success of these structures is heavily dependent on their interactions with their context: with the systems and people that provide resources and task, goal, and performance-related information to them (e.g., Ancona & Caldwell, 1992; Donnellon, 1996). When the organizational context in which teams operate is set up according to the old functional, hierarchical logic, teams can experience a great deal of difficulty. In her studies of new product development teams, Dougherty (1992) observed that failure to collaborate results in large part from differences in "thought worlds" stemming from the different knowledge bases and algorithms of different functional contributors and also from the routines that are built into hierarchical, functional organizations that tend to segment the work and perspectives of different contributors. She noted that successful teams created internal social systems that overcame the segmentation inherent in their organizational context and established new shared interpretations and processes.

In earlier work (Mohrman, Cohen & Mohrman, 1995) my colleagues and I have found that contextual organizational features in large part determine whether knowledge work teams are successful in carrying out their mission. These contextual features include direction-setting mechanisms (such as strategy and organizational goal-setting) and alignment mechanisms (the framework for organizational decision making, including clarity of authority) and performance management practices. Team difficulties often stem from tensions with organizational contexts that have been designed to support hierarchical, functional logic. For example, teams find themselves unable to carry out their tasks as planned because their functional hierarchy treats employees as interchangeable and pulls members wherever needed with little regard for the integrity of the team and its work. Rewards and appraisal are done by supervisors who apply standard functional criteria and have little visibility or concern for the work of the team. Members of the management team may be functionally oriented and provide little common framework for their reports, who are now working in a cross-functional world.

As a result of this research, we have argued that effective transition to an increasingly lateral logic and to doing work through lateral structures requires a redesign of many of the contextual features of the organization. Although hierarchy and concerns for functional excellence do not disappear because the organization is doing much of its work through lateral, cross-functional structures, these lateral structures require a reorientation of attention and a redefinition of responsibility. Members of successful lateral structures think about and are held accountable for the collective task, not just their piece of it. Their attention focuses on the needs and requirements of their team-mates with whom they are interdependent, not primarily on the wishes and desires of a hierarchical supervisor. Team members in effective teams learn together, develop mutual knowledge (Krauss & Fussell, 1990), develop mutual expectations about the nature of their task and how to work effectively as a team (Gabarro, 1990), and interrelate with one another in a manner that is "heedful" of each other's activities (Weick & Roberts, 1993).

This change to a lateral focus is difficult to achieve even in teams located within the same business unit and location. The challenge is even greater when geographically dispersed work structures are being utilized. To develop a fuller appreciation of the challenge of geographical dispersion, I depict a distributed team visually in a series of Figures that illustrate the layers of complexity that are entailed. Figure 5.1 shows a typical but simplified multi-site cross-functional new product development team. The "Hale-Bopp" project team is designing a sophisticated and rugged land-based portable telescope unit that can be moved from location to location and send images anywhere in the world. This is a task that requires the solution of a number of engineering design challenges. Additionally, in order to be commercially viable, the team has to find a way to manufacture this complex instrument with high levels of quality at near commodity prices. Time is critical because ongoing funding of core development activities depends on early demonstration of feasibility.

The project team consists of three sub-teams that are in three different locations. One sub-team is working on the software and firmware system, one on the hardware design, and the other on test and manufacturing processes. Even if the whole project team that is depicted in Figure 5.1 were in the same location, it would be quite challenged to operate successfully. It is a cross-functional unit whose members have highly honed and quite distinct knowledge sets but who have to work concurrently and interdependently with one another to meet the simultaneous goals of technological breakthroughs, cost, quality and speed. Thus there are discipline thought

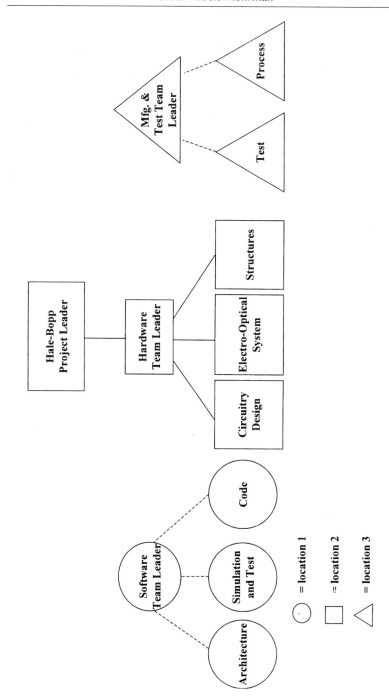

Figure 5.1 Distributed "Hale-Bopp" team project

worlds to bridge. Furthermore, all of the members of the software and manufacturing sub-teams are not fully dedicated to the Hale-Bopp project. Rather, they split time with at least one other project in their location. The Hale-Bopp project vies for attention with other projects.

Much of the work on distributed teams has focused on the project-level context that the team has to build in order to operate effectively. This includes a framework for communication and coordination, and norms and guidelines for using information technology to share information, coordinate the work and perform joint work with common data sets. It also includes roles and norms for decision making. Developing shared understanding of how the team will operate when distances are involved and different disciplines are located in different locations requires overcoming additional barriers. For example, in our studies, the attributions that are made by team members can seriously reduce team effectiveness. Commonly, software and hardware contributors devalue one another's work. Hardware contributors may attribute that software contributors aren't doing anything significant, based on their lack of visible concrete models, prototypes and product parameters that they are used to. The gap becomes even wider when these two groups are geographically dispersed and each group wants to wall itself off from intrusions from the other in order to be able to focus on their own part of the effort. There is also a tendency not to want to share work until it has been perfected, for fear of appearing incompetent (King *et al.*, 1998). These behaviors lead to further attributions that work is not being done. These dynamics led to members being unwilling to share information about work in progress in several cases that we studied, seriously impeding working relations and the ability of team members to work out their interdependencies. In one project team that we studied, for example, the software team leader proudly reported that he had instructed his team not to reply to queries from the other members of the team (who where in a different part of the country) because they could tolerate no delays in their work. He went so far as to wall off their files from the shared project information system so that hardware people couldn't independently look at their work and start critiquing or make incorrect assumptions. The lack of two-way information flow was estimated to have held up the overall project progress by two to three months.

Beyond these common process difficulties that reflect a lack of agreement regarding team strategy and the integrative context for doing work, our research has shown that the directional context in which teams operate is critical (Cohen, Mohrman & Mohrman, 1999). The team's ability to make the complex ongoing trade-offs required in such a development effort depends on its understanding of the organizational strategy and how this project fits in. Its ability to secure the resources and attention it needs from the larger organization depends on whether individual goals, team goals, and the goals of the larger business unit are aligned. Teams were more likely to have a clear directional context if the business unit management team provided consistent cross-functional direction. Otherwise various team members received conflicting messages from their functional heads about mission, purposes, and priorities of the team's project. When the managers above the team are also located in multiple locations, it is more difficult to provide consistent direction to the team members.

Figure 5.2 adds another level of complexity that makes it even more difficult to provide consistent direction. It turns out that the members of the Hale-Bopp project are organizationally located in different business units as well as in different locations. In fact, the production team is located in a different corporation, Make Co, that has a long term partnership with Elcomp, the corporation in which the hardware and software teams are located. Work on this project falls into three different business organizations and contextual frameworks: the sub-teams will be impacted by inconsistencies between the business objectives and priorities in the three organizations. For example, in one project team we studied, members of the hardware team were continually pulled away to deal with "bugs" in products already released to the field, because that was the bread and butter of the division that they belonged to. This totally frustrated the software team, whose members' time was fully dedicated to the project and who were well down the development path. The software division was the initiating division for the project and housed the overall project leader, and for this division the project was number one priority. Additionally, tensions between the partner manufacturing divisions and the project team emerged because the production company was unwilling to upgrade technology to deal with demanding performance and process sterility requirements. It viewed this project as a high risk project and could not internally justify additional project-specific investment that would not be needed for the other products they were manufacturing. The sub-teams in Hale-Bopp and in these other examples are embedded in business systems that have different business strategies, priorities, and investment plans. This makes it harder to achieve a consistent direction for the three sub-teams.

Figure 5.2 also illustrates the cross-cultural nature of the project team. Not only are the production engineers in the Hale-Bopp project in another company, they are also in another country with a substantially different culture. In many cases, this can lead not only to uncomfortable dynamics in the team, but also to fundamental cognitive misunderstandings that prevent coordinated knowledge work. In our studies, members of such teams talked frequently about getting together (by travelling or through teleconferencing) to work an issue, then thinking the issue had

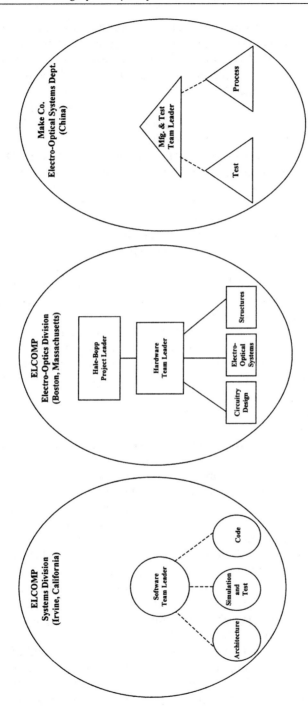

Figure 5.2 Distributed "Hale-Bopp" team nested in three businesses

been resolved but finding out weeks later that work had not proceeded the way any members of the team expected based on their experience of the working session. "We found out that we had not communicated at all", was a common sentiment expressed by team members. Cultural differences such as in formality, emphasis on hierarchy, and conflict avoidance or confrontation can exacerbate language differences and cause discomfort, lack of communication, and negative attributions that contribute to poor working relationships.

Figure 5.3 introduces yet more complexity to our team. It illustrates the different organizational structural contexts in which the subteams in the different locations are embedded. The organizational structures are different even between the two divisions of Elcomp. In the Systems Division (A), individual contributors report up through discipline managers. They are peers with the software team leader. In the Electro-Optical Division (B), the team members report to their team leader, who in turn reports into a programs organization. Team members have a weak dotted line relationship to the discipline managers. Although this may seem a small difference, we have found that reporting makes a large difference in terms of the consistency of the direction the team members receive and the priorities that pervade the organization. When team members report for operational purposes to a manager outside the team, they are frequently subject to many pressures for performance that distract from and may even interfere with the work of the team. Another seemingly subtle difference that can cause great difficulties for teams is illustrated by the Make Co structure. Make Co team members have solid line reporting up a long hierarchical chain, a configuration that reflects the hierarchical nature of decision making and the relative lack of decision making authority within the manufacturing subteam. This makes it difficult or impossible for the Hale-Bopp project team to resolve issues on-line and introduces delays and uncertainty into their work.

There are a number of other contextual differences that greatly impact the Hale-Bopp team. In the systems division, for example, the software team leader is also the leader for two other software development programs, and the same individuals are executing all three. Their attention is continually shifting between projects. The members of the hardware team are dedicated full-time to the Hale-Bopp project. The test and process members in Make Co have this project as one collateral assignment—the majority of their job is spent managing internal projects and workflow within Make Co. Whereas Hale-Bopp is the second highest priority project within the Electro-Optical Division, it is in the lower half of priorities for the Systems Division, which is a relatively new division and is most fixated on releasing it's own stand-alone systems products. The Systems Division is supporting the Electro-Optical Division because of corporate

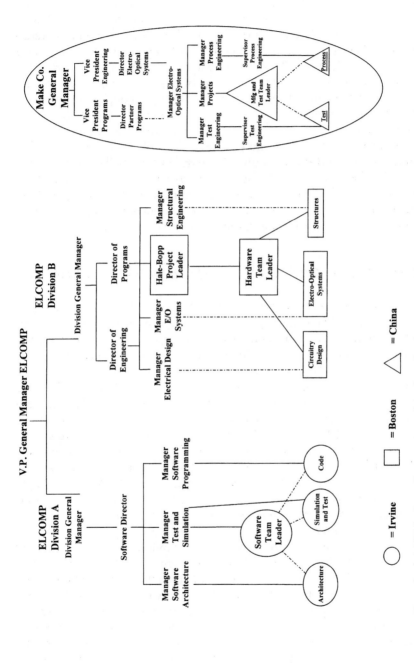

Figure 5.3 Distributed "Hale-Bopp" team nested in three business structures

citizenship requirements. In Make Co, Hale-Bopp is one of ten product development activities that vie for attention with each other and with fifteen products in current manufacturing. The terms of the partnership agreement dictate that Make Co receives no revenue for Hale-Bopp until it goes into production. Thus, the overarching business logic and structure of each organization and the terms of their relationship to one another are key contextual factors impacting the Hale-Bopp project team.

As mentioned earlier, contextual factors are critical facilitators of, or barriers to, performance in all lateral structures. Geographically distributed teams are subject to an even more complex set of contexts that include cultural and business unit diversity. Furthermore, their primary mode of interaction is not through face-to-face interactions, making it more difficult to work out conflicts, determine shared meaning, and develop an agreed-to framework for operating. Some of the implications for practice and theory are briefly discussed in the next section.

IMPLICATIONS FOR ORGANIZATION BEHAVIOR AND DESIGN

Working across boundaries is becoming a key capability in today's organizations. Projects like Hale-Bopp are becoming routine in many organizations, which means that individuals collaborate across distances, cultures, organizations, and disciplines. Given the contextual complexity of such work, a key imperative in today's world is to develop new models of organization and learn how to create contexts within which distributed work can occur more naturally. This conclusion is not new. Much writing about new organizational forms has stressed their boundaryless nature (e.g., Galbraith & Lawler, 1994). However, much existing writing simply describes these emerging work structures without delving deeply into the contextual features that have to be developed to elicit the fundamentally different kind of organizational behavior that they require. The fields of organizational behavior and theory will have to grapple with many new questions and foster new models for explaining behavior that can deal with this new reality.

In discussing this, I will not dwell on the obvious and very important issues of developing, implementing and learning how to operate effectively across distances with new electronic tools for collaboration. In addition to those issues that have to do with the means of work, at least four major issues of organization context need to be addressed in order to create widespread organizational capability to work effectively through distributed teams. These have to do with governance structures, context-building, lateral and vertical context management, and the development of human resource systems to fit the new contexts for work. The tension in all four of these areas is between the need for these lateral structures to clearly fit within their organizational contexts in order to achieve ongoing support, and at the same time to be de-coupled from those contexts.

Governance Structures

Traditional governance structures have relied primarily on hierarchy. Mission, strategy, resource allocation, much operational decision-making and ultimate accountability have lain with the top management of the corporation. The last two decades have seen an increase in emphasis on decentralization of operational and performance accountability to self-contained business units and increased self-management for operational issues. Recent attention to quality management and process reengineering have made salient the need to purposively manage the lateral processes of the organization in order to assure effective and efficient delivery of value to the customer, and to place decision authority in units that operate laterally. This attention to the lateral dimension of organizing has yielded tension within organizations about how to manage across parts of the organization when the dominant systems and processes support traditional vertical hierarchical control (Lawler & Mohrman, 1998).

The use of geographically dispersed teams, and teams that cut across business units and corporations, underscores the need to find governance approaches that enable lateral self-management. The Hale-Bopp project, for example, is reliant on three different businesses for resources and ongoing support, and on three different hierarchical structures for decision approval. Rather than yielding agility and flexibility, in our studies such structures were likely to spend a great deal of time slogging through endless issues of contextual conflict and uncertainty. If we assume that each of the three businesses involved in this project are simultaneously involved in a number of other complicated, lateral projects, the amount of time spent in each organization working the context can become overwhelming.

The effectiveness of all teams relates to the consistency and continuity of the direction they receive from their management structure. The challenge posed by Hale-Bopp and other similar projects is to set up an inter-organizational governance framework to provide integrated direction to the distributed team. Distributed projects are alliances, in which different units combine resources in order to meet a market need that they could not independently address. Alliances require agreement about governance, generally through some sort of joint process. They also require a clear agreement about the resources that various parties will provide and their accountabilities to one another. It is this governance framework that creates the umbrella within which the operating parties of the alliance can

carry out their tasks with reliable support and minimal day-to-day interference from the various businesses that are party to the alliances. Clarify-
ing governance connects these dispersed projects to the mission of each of
the business units and simultaneously creates a framework for them to
operate independently.

Experience with joint ventures and other forms of alliance provides
models for inter-organizational governance structures. In the future, we
can expect to see organizations learning how to spawn, and collaboratively and efficiently govern, many dispersed and often temporary
activities. This represents a continuation of the trend toward more lateral
self-management in the organization.

Context-Building

Each dispersed project has a unique configuration of activities and participants. The project level context and the larger organizational and inter-
organizational contexts in which the project is embedded are also unique.
Thus, managers and project leaders and participants need to learn to
create effective performance contexts. The organizational design no
longer can be simply the backdrop for work; it has to be intentionally
crafted to house complex, virtual work.

Organizational level design features that affect lateral, distributed
work, include the information system infrastructure, communication
norms and systems, planning, goal-setting, and budgeting processes, and
measurement, review, and reward systems (Galbraith, 1994). These systems provide an integrative framework for a myriad of dispersed, multi-
dimensional activities. When the dispersed team cuts across organizations, inter-organizational integration of these systems is required in
order to align performers who don't fall within the same hierarchical
structure.

These contextual features to some extent substitute for hierarchical
control: they are the features that both connect teams to the larger business units in which the members are embedded and allow the teams to
operate in a loosely coupled manner. For example, strategy, planning,
and goal-setting processes are important for all lateral structures, for it is
through these mechanisms that various units become aligned with the
overall business direction and have a clear framework within which to
make trade-offs and guide their own activities (Cohen, Mohrman &
Mohrman, 1998). Information sharing ensures that the team has the
necessary knowledge of events in each organizational unit to make informed decisions that take their context into account. These factors are
even more important for dispersed teams, because relying on the process
of hierarchical control and decision-making is much too cumbersome

given the complexity of the hierarchical structure and the dynamic nature of the environment.

Project participants must also craft a within-project context. This context includes internal norms, processes, and structures for coordination and collaboration, working across cultural and discipline divides, and for self-management. As projects go through various stages and different participants become involved, the context is reshaped continually. The tools of project management increasingly include organization design.

Managers and leaders in the effective teams in our studies had gravitated away from day-to-day management of team member activities. They spent time building contexts for effective performance. Contextual features were the determinants of team performance. Classic managerial variables dealing with the dyadic relationship between managers and subordinates explained very little of the variance in performance. In the future, project management will be a key managerial competency, and all managers will have to know how to build organizational contexts and temporary systems.

Lateral and Vertical Context Management

In addition to the new behaviors and competencies required to effectively operate within distributed teams, the members of these teams will have to become quite good at managing their complex contexts. Distributed team members often have additional responsibilities outside the team and often as members of other teams as well. They have to become comfortable with the ambiguity and uncertainty of juggling multiple priorities with no one clear source of direction about what are the most important activities. They have to be able to negotiate a path through a complex maze of loosely coupled or uncoupled activities and demands on their time. In a sense, each individual is a supplier of services, juggling multiple commitments.

Teams have to manage their relations laterally as well as with multiple hierarchies. Often the interdependencies inherent in knowledge work extend beyond a particular team. Minimally, other teams are the source of important knowledge content. Multiple teams may also be vying for scarce shared resources, and consequently coordination is required. The various participants in a distributed team operate within different organizational contexts, and the team is dependent on support and cooperation from each. Keeping "all the ducks in line" is a major concern, and requires negotiation and collaboration skills as well as a project management approach that includes ongoing alignment of needed contextual support in order to ensure that the team can operate without external interference.

Human Resource Systems

Traditional human resource systems have been crafted to support hierarchical functioning and are based on the assumption that work is done within a particular organization. Career paths have largely been viewed as vertical movement through an organization. Performance management systems have largely used the supervisor–subordinate relationship as their core building block. Job assignments have been within a particular organizational unit and setting. Compensation has been geared to particular jobs within particular organizational structures. Team and organizational rewards, when they exist, often target the performance of a particular business unit or team within it.

Individuals working in dispersed teams can feel at risk when such traditional approaches prevail. Their work may not be salient nor perhaps even visible to their supervisor or even to others in their business unit. The project may be of relatively low priority to the business unit in which they are located but of high priority in the larger business context. Their assignments may not fall neatly within the job structure of their own organization.

As dispersed teams become more prevalent, organizations will have to find ways to plan job assignments, assess competency and value, provide feedback, and reward units that do not depend on the traditional supervisory structure as the agent of performance and career management. We can expect to see an increasing use of reward structures that are project specific and link together members from diverse businesses. Individuals will develop portfolios of experience and project-based assessments that will become the basis for job assignments through processes that resemble market mechanisms more closely than traditional hierarchically controlled people movement. These mechanisms will increasingly extend across business units within a corporation, and may even start to extend across multiple organizations that have teams that cut across them. Thus, the attachment of people to their company will be through the projects of which they are a part; those projects will also provide a forum for applying one's competencies that is relatively detached from day-to-day concern with vertical hierarchical person management. One's accomplishments and the accomplishments of the projects will be the basis for further opportunities.

This change will also have profound implications for roles and relationships in the organization. Managers will truly become managers of activities rather than people. Self-reliance and self-management will be critical to career success. Business units will no longer "own" their people—rather, mechanisms will develop to facilitate the application of people's talent to projects that extend across the corporation. Locations will house people and provide administrative support, but direction, resources, project management and co-workers may come from anywhere.

CONCLUSION

For compelling business reasons, geographically dispersed, multi-organization project teams and networks are becoming increasingly prevalent in many organizations. These structures exist in multiple organizational and often cultural contexts, and entail a dramatically more complex set of operating constraints than is true for project teams located together in the same organizational unit. For these dispersed structures to deliver on their business potential, organizations will have to build contexts that at the same time link these teams to the multiple business units of which their members are a part and umbrella them from daily interference by these business units.

Dispersed teams and networks are a way of organizing work that challenges many of the assumptions and approaches of the traditional hierarchical business model. New lateral forms of governance are required, as well as systems and contextual features that enable work to occur with relative ease across boundaries. These new forms in turn will have significant implications for organizational behavior and for human resource management approaches because they challenge the traditional attachment of people to the organization primarily through well-defined jobs and supervisor–subordinate relations.

REFERENCES

Ancona, D. G. & Caldwell, D. F. (1992) Bridging the boundary: external activity and performance in organizational teams. *Administrative Science Quarterly*, **37**: 634–665.

Cohen, S. G., Mohrman, S. A. & Mohrman, A. M. (1999) We can't get there unless we know where we are going: direction setting for knowledge work teams. In R. Wageman (Ed.) *Research on Groups and Teams*. Greenwich, CT: JAI Press, pp. 1–31.

Davenport, T. H. & Prusak, L. (1998) *Working Knowledge: How Organizations Manage What they Know*. Boston, Mass.: Harvard Business School Press.

Donnellon, A. (1996) *Team Talk: Listening Between the Lines to Improve Team Performance*. Cambridge, Mass.: Harvard Business School Press.

Dougherty, D. (1992) Interpretive barriers to successful product innovation in large firms. *Organization Science*, 3(2): 179–202.

Ferranti, M. (1997) Automaker aims for companywide collaborative standards. *Computing*. **December 11.**

Gabarro, J. (1990) The development of working relationships. In J. Galegher, R. E. Kraus & C. Egido (Eds) *Intellectual Teamwork: The Social and Technological Bases of Cooperative Work*. Hillsdale, NJ: Erlbaum, pp. 79–110.

Galbraith, J. R. (1994) *Competing with Flexible Lateral Organizations*. Reading, Mass.: Addison-Wesley.

Galbraith, J. R. & Lawler, E. E. III (Eds) (1994) *Organizing for the Future: The New Logic for Managing Complex Organizations*. San Francisco: Jossey-Bass.

Galegher, J., Kraut, R. E. & Egido, C. (Eds) (1990) *Intellectual Teamwork: The Social and Technological Bases of Cooperative Work*. Hillsdale, NJ: Erlbaum.

Huber, G. P. (1990) A theory of the effects of advanced information technologies on organizational design, intelligence, and decision making. *The Academy of Management Review*, **19**(1): 47–71.

Lawler, E. & Mohrman, S. (1998) Employee involvement, reengineering, and TQM: focusing on capability development. In S. A. Mohrman, J. A. Galbraith & E. E. Lawler III (Eds) *Tomorrow's Organization: Crafting Winning Capabilities in a Dynamic World*. San Francisco, CA: Jossey-Bass, pp. 179–207.

Jarvenpaa, S. L. & Ives, B. (1994) The global network organization of the future: information management opportunities and challenges, *Journal of Management Information Systems*, **10**(4): 25–54.

Johansen, R. (1999) *Groupware: Computer Support for Business Teams*. New York: Free Press.

King, N., Rice, R. E., Majchrsak, A., Malhotra, A. & Ba, S. (1998) Computer-mediated inter-organizational knowledge-sharing: insights from a virtual team innovating using a collaborative tool. Technical Report, Los Angeles: The University of Southern California.

Krauss, R. & Fussell, S. (1990) Mutual knowledge and communicative effectiveness. In J. Galegher, R. E. Kraus & C. Egido (Eds), *Intellectual Teamwork: The Social and Technological Bases of Cooperative Work*. Hillsdale, NJ: Erlbaum.

Mohrman, S. A., Cohen, S. G. & Mohrman, A. M., Jr. (1995) *Designing Team-based Organizations: New Applications for Knowledge Work*. San Francisco: Jossey-Bass.

Tenkasi, R., Mohrman, S. A. & Mohrman, A. M. (1998) Accelerating organizational learning during transition. In Mohrman, S. A., Galbraith, J. R., Lawler, E. III *et al.*, *Tomorrow's Organizations: Crafting Winning Capabilities in a Dynamic World*. San Francisco: Jossey-Bass.

Weick, K. E. & Roberts, K. H. (1993) Collective mind in organizations: heedful interrelating on flight decks. *Administrative Science Quarterly*, **38**: 357–381.

CHAPTER 6

Interdependence in Virtual Organizations

Gerardine DeSanctis, Nancy Staudenmayer and Sze Sze Wong
Fuqua School of Business, Duke University, Box 90120, Durham, NC 27708, USA

INTRODUCTION

As we approach the start of a new millenium, a variety of forces are converging and fostering the emergence of so-called virtual forms of organizing. Some of these forces are internally driven and reflect changes in the composition of organizations and the nature of the work they perform. For example, the members of organizations are more diverse, and their work is more knowledge-based and service-oriented. Some forces are the consequence of environmental factors such as more rapid product cycles, increased inter-organizational cooperation and global competition. Still other forces are rooted in technology, particularly information technology. Innovations such as the Internet, World Wide Web, and software agents are infusing organizations and enabling new capabilities. As a result, many organizations are working in more distributed, and more time and technology intensive, ways (Bleeker, 1994; Davidow & Malone, 1992; Fulk & DeSanctis, 1995).

Paralleling the emergence of the "virtual organization" is a growing consensus in organization theory that a more relational view, which conceptualizes firms as networks of internal and external ties, is preferred over more traditional models of organizations (Ghoshal & Bartlett, 1990; Ibarra, 1992; Masciarelli, 1998). Network theorists point out that actions are embedded in systems of ongoing economic and social relations (Granovetter, 1985). Rather than focusing solely on the attributes of atomic individuals or firms, network studies highlight the role a nodal unit's position plays within a network—showing, for example, how

Trends in Organizational Behavior, Volume 6. Edited by C. L. Cooper and D. M. Rousseau.
Copyright © 1999 John Wiley & Sons, Ltd.

structural variables such as the density, strength, formality, or multiplicity of ties yield outcomes such as social capital, trust, or learning (Brass, 1984; Ibarra & Andrews, 1993; Powell, 1990; Uzzi, 1997). While greatly enhancing our understanding of organizations, the research thus far has exhibited a strong sociological bias. We need to also consider networks from the perspective of organization design and coordination. For example, how do managers resolve the conflict inherent in trying to coordinate multiple relationships over time? How does the existence of multiple networked relations create opportunities and constraints on action?

A complementary perspective to understanding the virtual form, grounded in activities and relationships, is the concept of *interdependence*. At its most basic level, interdependence refers to a state of being in which an entity (such as a person, organizational unit, or firm) is determined, influenced, or controlled by some other entity.[1] Interdependence, therefore, lies at the very heart of what an organization is and why organizations exist (Barnard, 1948). Like network theory, concepts of interdependence involve understanding relationships, but the richness of the concept, supported by a long history of research that spans disciplines, makes it a particularly useful and appropriate way to study virtual organizations. In particular, this lens enables us to differentiate ties in ways standard network theory cannot. For example, interdependence most often appears in theories of organization design to account for the central paradox that tasks must be decomposed and then integrated across entities (March & Simon, 1958; Lawrence & Lorsch, 1967). But the concept is also a central component in theories of relationship management, which examine how people depend on one another for mutual support and intrinsic or extrinsic resources (Kelley & Thibault, 1978; Pfeffer & Salancik, 1978; Rusbult, 1983, 1986; Thibault & Kelley, 1959). Emerging research in social cognition likewise draws upon the concept to explain the interdependence of individual knowledge and memory structures (Wegner, 1986; Wegner *et al.*, 1985; Wegner *et al.*, 1991; Weick & Roberts, 1993).

Although the management of interdependence is not new, the amount, nature, and process of managing interdependencies is increasingly important in today's business environment. As firms become more distributed in time and space, more linked across functions and with other firms, and more cross-cultural—in other words, more virtual-management of interdependent relationships becomes enormously challenging. New research questions such as the following arise: How do the number and nature of interdependencies change as organizations move from traditional multidivisional structures to more virtual forms? As external ties like strategic

---

[1] In this paper we use the term interdependence comprehensively to include both dependent (one-way) and interdependent (two-way) interactions.

alliances and partnerships are created and destroyed, what are the associated impacts on interdependencies among teams and individuals inside the firm? How do new forms of technology enable the creation, dissolution, and tracking of new and old interdependencies over time? Most fundamentally, how do firms, groups, and individuals manage the portfolio of different interdependencies characteristic of virtual organizations? Which interdependencies do they choose to pursue, which do they ignore, and how do they cope with the potential conflict among interdependencies, not to mention the information, time, and emotional overload?

Our aim in this paper is to show how the concept of interdependence might be applied to the study of virtual organizations in order to start addressing these and related questions. We begin by briefly describing virtual organizations and contrasting them with more traditional forms of organizing. We then review the concept of interdependence and illustrate how its application yields insight into the management challenges confronting virtual firms at the organizational, workgroup, and individual levels. We conclude by examining the various roles technology plays in the management of interdependencies in virtual settings. We argue that just as relationships infuse the virtual organization and require taking a broad-based view of the concept, the pervasiveness of technology in virtual settings requires the integration of multiple perspectives. By focusing on interdependency and its management, we hope to expand current perspectives on virtual organizing, and hence stimulate future research in this area.

VIRTUAL ORGANIZATIONS

The possibility of the virtual corporation is one of the most exciting propositions to arrive on the management scene in recent years. Offering sleek, highly efficient and customized global commerce with a flexible, distributed workforce, the virtual corporation raises both hopes and fears as organizations confront the challenges of the 21st century. Whereas traditional firms operate within well-defined departments, divisions, or business units, virtual firms conduct their work activities across the confines of time, space, culture, and organizational boundary (Hedberg et al., 1997).

Even though the virtual organization is widely discussed in both business and academic circles, a definitive description of the virtual form has yet to appear. Nonetheless, the virtual organization is often defined as one that is interspersed with external ties (Coyle & Schnarr, 1995; King, 1994), managed with an internal structure of virtual teams that are assembled and disassembled according to need (Lipnack & Stamps, 1997; McDonald, 1995; Simons, 1995) and consisting of employees who are frequently physically dispersed from one another (Clancy, 1994; Barner,

1996). The result is a "company without walls" (Galbraith, 1995) that acts as a "collaborative network of people" working together, regardless of location and who "owns" them (Bleeker, 1994). Proponents of this new form extol its benefits in terms of greater adaptability, faster response time, and task specialization, while critics argue the potential downsides, including greater conflict, decreased firm loyalty, and higher probability of catastrophic effects (see Burris, 1993).

Despite the media hyperbole, few pure virtual forms exist today (Dutton, 1999). Instead, we see aspects of virtuality in many business enterprises. For example, although most companies still maintain a divisional structure and high levels of vertical as opposed to horizontal integration, they are increasingly forming external relationships with other firms in the form of strategic partnerships, alliances, and outsourcing contracts (Mowshowitz, 1994; Nohria & Berkley, 1994). Likewise, although teams are largely composed of internal employees, there is movement towards more geographically distributed and cross-functional teams (Ancona & Caldwell, 1987). In addition, rapid advancement in telecommunications has enabled more telecommuting and cooperation among physically distributed employees (Barner, 1996; King, 1994). Taken overall, these trends suggest that firms are investing more heavily in interdependent relationships than in the past and taking on more virtual characteristics (Davidow & Malone, 1992).

Thus, the virtual organization may not be so much a pure form as a continuum for describing a range of relationships along the dimensions of space, time, culture, and organizational boundary (see Figure 6.1). To the extent that the relationships of a firm take on more and more of these characteristics, the firm is relatively more virtual. Being virtual, therefore, is a matter of degree (Kraut *et al.*, in press), and even firms that may not look virtual at the surface are acting virtual in some aspects of their management.

INTERDEPENDENCE

The virtual firm has been described as a network of interdependencies, and the management of these interdependencies is cited as a key challenge (Davidow & Malone, 1992; Jarillo, 1993; Lockett & Holland, 1996). In order to understand the implications of the virtual organization for interdependency management, it is perhaps helpful to review some of the basic aspects of the concept.[2]

---

[2] This review is not representative of the entire literature on interdependence in organizations. For more comprehensive discussions see McCann and Ferry (1979) or Staudenmayer (1997). Major theoretical and empirical studies include Thompson (1967), Pfeffer and Salancik (1978), Mitchell and Silver (1990), Gresov (1990), and Wageman (1995).

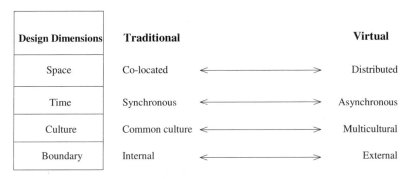

Design Dimensions	Traditional		Virtual
Space	Co-located	⟵————————⟶	Distributed
Time	Synchronous	⟵————————⟶	Asynchronous
Culture	Common culture	⟵————————⟶	Multicultural
Boundary	Internal	⟵————————⟶	External

Figure 6.1 Relative to the traditional organization, relationships in the virtual organization are more geographically distributed, more asynchronous, more multicultural, and more likely to extend outside the firm.

In contrast to work that is managed independently, interdependent work occurs when one node in the organizational network is reliant on another, or vice versa. Depending on the level of analysis, the node might be an individual, group, department, business unit, firm, or even collection of firms. The basis for interdependence is usually portrayed as task completion, but interdependence can reflect contingencies involving shared goals or rewards, or even a combination of behavior and outcomes. Interdependence is typically operationalized as communication or the exchange of task-related information (Thompson, 1967; Tushman, 1979) but has also been conceptualized as representing the degree of need for an intrinsic or extrinsic resource (Kelley & Thibault, 1978; March & Simon, 1958; Pfeffer & Salancik, 1978; Thibault & Kelley, 1959) or tacit knowledge structures (Wegner, 1986; Wegner et al., 1985; Wegner et al., 1991; Weick & Roberts, 1993).

Not too surprisingly, given this breadth of application and perspective, interdependence has been studied along a number of different dimensions. Interdependencies can be differentiated in terms of their *structure* (sequential, pooled, reciprocal, team, network) (Thompson, 1967; Van de Ven, Delbecq & Koenig, 1976); *complexity* (the number of nodes involved); *formality* (degree to which exchange procedures are specified in advance); and *symmetry* (degree to which power is equally distributed across nodes). (See Ebers, 1997; Granovetter, 1985; Staudenmayer, 1997 and Tjosvold, 1986 for review of these and other dimensions.)

The fusion of an old concept (interdependence) with a new applied setting (virtual organizations) also calls for a re-examination of the traditional approaches to understanding interdependence and identification of potential new ones (see Figure 6.2). For example, the study of interdependence traditionally has centered either on transactions—i.e., isolated

TRADITIONAL ORGANIZATIONS	VIRTUAL ORGANIZATIONS
Transactions *or* relationships	Transactions *and* relationships
Single dimension	Multiple dimensions
Static	Dynamic and evolving
Single level	Cross level
Stripped of context	Interdependencies within a given business, social, and temporal context
Organization Design as "fitting" structure to isolated, static interdependence	Organization Design as management of multiple interdependent relationships

Figure 6.2 Approaches to the study of interdependence in traditional versus virtual organizations

information or resource exchange, communication, or contract management—or on relationships—i.e., ongoing interaction among parties within a social context. The virtual environment of today requires integrating transactional and relational perspectives insofar as virtual organizations embody both poles of the continuum. For instance, how do social relationships enable or hinder the formation or dissolution of task-based interdependencies? Alternatively, do symmetrical interdependencies involving shared cognition serve as the basis for more long lasting relationships?

As firms move toward the virtual form, their interdependencies are likely to go up in the aggregate but also may increase differentially. Interdependence research in the past has tended to focus on one type of interdependence at a time—the structure of internal information processing interdependencies, for instance. The new relationship–intensive context demands adopting more multidimensional perspectives of interdependence, which draw upon and integrate what are typically seen as isolated theories. Both internal interdependencies (across intra-firm boundaries) and external interdependencies (across inter-firm boundaries) are of interest, as are those based on information processing and resource sharing.

Interdependencies may also dynamically spread downward, upward, or across the virtual firm such that, at any given point in time, the presence of interdependencies in one part of the organization may not necessarily imply equivalent interdependencies in other parts of the firm. For example, formation of a strategic alliance at the corporate level may lead to interdependencies among the departments, teams, and individual workers in the firm that are involved in the larger alliance relationship (Eccles & Crane, 1988). In the same vein, individuals, teams, or departments that work closely with say, suppliers, to develop products that fulfill special customer needs may, in the long run, be creating interdependencies that lead to future corporate-level partnerships. In this way, formation of interdependencies can cascade down in the firm (from top management to individual workers) or up (from individual workers to the top management level). The number of interdependencies may also increase laterally if formation of relationships between one department or business unit and an external party encourages the spread of similar relationships to other parts of the firm. These interdependencies are likely to vary considerably in terms of their basis for formation, structure, complexity, formality, etc. Figure 6.3 illustrates the spectrum of interdependencies that are relevant to the study of virtual organizations.

A critical implication is that researchers studying virtual organizations need to look beyond corporate-level alliances and partnerships to consider the dynamics of interdependencies at and among the organizational, work group, and individual levels of analysis. Whereas previous approaches tended to examine interdependence stripped of context, future research in virtual organizations will need to understand interdependencies within a business, social, and temporal context.

Finally, the interdependent network view analyzes the firm less as a set of boxes, connections, and boundaries and more as a "seamless web" of activities within a continually shifting context (Eccles & Crane, 1988). The configuration of the firm is depicted as fluid and dynamic, held together through an array of coordination mechanisms ranging from traditional control systems to self-designing structures. The process of organization design therefore shifts from an emphasis on static architectures to a focus on the continuous formation and maintenance of internal and external relationships. Likewise, the analytical challenge is less one of "fitting" structure to a particular situation and more about understanding the dynamic interplay between changes in interdependent relationships and changes in form (e.g., how new relationships necessitate design changes and how new designs enable or inhibit the development of relationships) (Eccles & Nohria, 1992).

Interdependency provides a useful conceptual lens through which to examine the changes that organizations experience as they take on virtual characteristics. We can generate hypotheses about the precise ways in which organizations will change as they become more virtual. We can also pinpoint the kinds of managerial dilemmas and challenges that firms will confront as they operate in virtual mode and start to generate new possibilities for managing the complexities of web-like, relational forms.

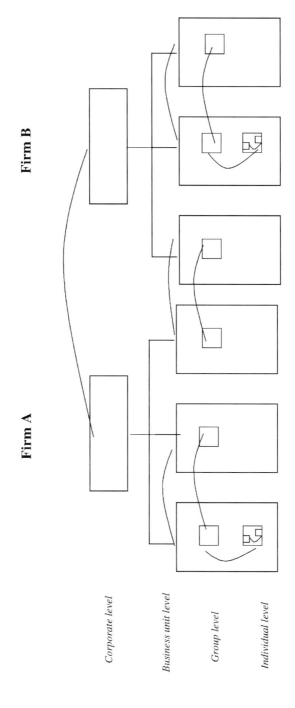

Figure 6.3 Interdependencies in the virtual organization can occur both internally and externally and at various levels of the firm.

We illustrate this process in the next section by describing how interdependencies are likely to change—and, in the process, change worklife—at three levels of analysis: organization, workgroup, and individual.

IMPLICATIONS OF INTERDEPENDENCE

Changes in Organization-Level Interdependence

Figure 6.4 summarizes changes in interdependencies that might be expected as firms become more virtual.

Number of Interdependencies

Since the formation of boundary-spanning relationships is the very essence of the virtual form, the *number* of interdependencies in the firm should increase, and these interdependencies will tend to form not only between groups, units, and departments but also across the external boundaries of each entity and the firm at large.

Type and Nature of Interdependencies

As the trend towards globalization continues unabated and as inter-organizational cooperative ventures continue to proliferate, firms are likely to be embedded in complex webs of *external* ties. This being said, the relative proportion of external to internal interdependencies may vary depending on the stage of the firm and the nature of the work it performs. For example, initial high levels of external interdependence may, over time, yield a complex network of internal interdependencies to support the external relationships (Eccles & Crane, 1988).

The proportion of *lateral* interdependent relationships (whether internal or external) should increase relative to vertical interdependencies (Victor & Blackburn, 1978) as firms bring decision making closer to the point of execution. The move toward lateral coordination strategies, in turn, implies greater *symmetry* among the parties involved in any given interdependency and creates the opportunity for more complexity and flexibility in the design of the relationship. Over time, we might expect simple input/output exchanges to be replaced by more *complex* structures such as reciprocal, team-based, and network patterns (Van de Ven, Delbecq & Koenig, 1976).

Furthermore, since tasks in the virtual firm are often knowledge-based, we would expect to see more interdependencies based on the sharing of intellectual as opposed to physical *resources*. In order to hedge against

---

As Firms Become More Virtual...

The overall *number* of interdependencies in the firm will increase.

The proportion of *external* interdependencies will increase relative to internal interdependencies (at least temporarily).

The proportion of *lateral* interdependencies will increase relative to vertical interdependencies.

There will be greater *symmetry* in interdependencies.

The proportion of *structurally complex* interdependencies (e.g., reciprocal, team, network) will increase relative to structurally simple interdependencies (e.g., input/output, sequential)

The *resources* exchanged in interdependencies will be more knowledge and skill-based rather than material or monetary based.

Interdependencies will become shorter in *duration* (although embedded in ongoing relationships).

The proportion of *unanticipated* interdependencies will increase relative to routine interdependencies.

Figure 6.4   Anticipated changes in interdependencies as firms become more virtual

uncertainty and/or to exploit future opportunities, organizations are more likely to cultivate short-term or temporary interdependencies, which offer the option of dissolving or redesigning the relationship at some future point in time. The average *duration* of interdependencies, therefore, may decline. Even though each interdependent relationship may span a shorter period of time, this does not imply that the social relationship that has arisen, by way of the interdependency, has dissolved as well. On the contrary, the social relationship may continue to persist, and could be evoked when the need arises to create a new interdependent relationship of a different nature.

If firms rely on more knowledge-based interdependencies of shorter duration, one implication is that interdependencies may become more *unanticipated* in virtual organizations. Interdependencies traditionally have been thought of as being explicit and anticipatable, that is, formally recognized by the organization and the parties involved, with few risks of surprises. Attempts to model workflow, create task designs, and develop written job descriptions exemplify efforts to explicate interdependencies, and to minimize the unexpected. But some interdependencies always remain unanticipated or outside the immediate view (or awareness) of participants and observers (Staudenmayer, 1997). In the virtual organization, unanticipated interdependencies may emerge in order to "get the job done" when prespecified relationships either fail or prove inadequate for meeting short-term work goals. Unanticipated interdependencies also may exist when individuals are not cognizant of constraints or opportunities outside their area of expertise. For example, product development specialists working on one component of a new product may inadvertently create interdependencies with other units of the firm when making product design decisions. The likelihood of creating such unanticipated interdependencies is higher in virtual organizations because they tend to be flat, decentralized, and reliant on specialized knowledge bases and rapidly changing interactions. Fluidity in organization design and turbulence in the external environment also add to the possibility of unanticipated interdependencies, because they render obsolete many traditional assumptions about others' actions and constraints.

Changes in Workgroup-Level Interdependence

Teams constitute the core work entity of the virtual firm, the "basic building block" of what it means to organize in virtual mode (Davidow & Malone, 1992; Dutton, 1999; Jarvenpaa & Shaw, 1998; Lipnack & Stamps, 1997). In traditional organizations, team members are co-located, meet face-to-face, and come from similar companies or business units with common cultural backgrounds. In such settings, interdependencies can be managed by assigning permanent members to the team, establishing relatively fixed roles, and developing work routines. As a team becomes virtual, its membership is likely to become more cross-functional, more geographically dispersed, more culturally diverse, and more temporary (Jarvenpaa & Leidner, in press). These shifts imply important changes in interdependence as well as the very nature of teamwork (Figure 6.5).

Type and Nature of Interdependencies

Since virtual team members are scattered, they are more likely to form relationships outside the team, so the number of *external* interdependencies is likely to increase. Pressures to integrate the team's work with the

---

As Teams Become More Virtual...

The number of *external* interdependencies will increase.

Interdependencies will become more *dynamic* due to greater decentralization and switching of tasks, roles, and assignments.

Overall, the *variety* of interdependence at the team level will increase.

Interdependencies among team members will become more *visible* inside and outside the team but at the same time the incidence of "hidden" interdependence will increase.

The above changes imply that:

Membership in the team will become less clear.

Structural arrangements will become more *temporary* and less *routinized*.

Average team *life span* will shorten.

There will be greater *loss of privacy* due to higher visibility of interdependence and more frequent interruptions.

Cohesion and trust within the team will be more difficult to maintain.

Figure 6.5 Anticipated changes in interdependencies and their implications as teams become more virtual

firm at large and to link with customers or others outside the organization also increase the likelihood of growth in external interdependencies. Since every group member is a potential node of connectivity to an external party, relationships can form rapidly, often without formal planning or managerial intent.

In line with general organizational trends toward more lateral, symmetrical, and temporary ties, the interdependencies experienced by teams are likely to be highly *dynamic*. Greater switching of tasks, roles, or work assignments should be possible in the virtual team. This allows what Mowshowitz calls "combinatorial freedom," or the ability to allocate work across people or subgroups of people depending on workload demands (Mowshowitz, 1994). If teams take on multiple tasks, the structure of interdependence may vary across tasks. For example, a team may use a formal, sequential approach to managing customer complaints and an informal, reciprocal approach to solving personnel conflicts. We would therefore expect greater *varieties* of interdependence within and across virtual teams in terms of nodal arrangements and other dimensions.

Interdependencies among members of virtual teams may become more *visible* to both team members and outsiders than in the past. In distributed teams, members are more likely to rely on documents, mail messages, and written forms of information exchange rather than face-to-face discussions or informal meetings. For example, teams may use electronic document systems, stored bulletin-board notes, or share copies of their e-mail messages. People on the inside of the group may see copies of documents or messages exchanged among team members and so become aware of interdependencies (or some aspects of the interdependencies) as they arise. If these kinds of products of interdependent relationships are archived or made available to outsiders, it is possible that parties external to the team may more readily observe how work in the team is coordinated, formalized, negotiated, and so on. On the other hand, the decentralized and dynamic nature of work in virtual teams suggests that some interdependencies may remain "hidden" from full group consciousness (Staudenmayer, 1997).

The long-term implications of these sorts of changes for the nature of teamwork may be complicated and difficult to anticipate. As individuals make links between the group and other groups it could become difficult to identify who is in the group, who is out, and where the borders of group *membership* begin and end. Virtual teams may grow and shrink depending on the task at hand or the *ad hoc* choices by group members about whom to include or exclude from group activities. Structural arrangements will tend to be more *temporary*, *routinization* of work less likely, and the team's *life span* may shorten. Teams may be created and destroyed depending on the larger demands of the organization or the environment.

Some teams may experience a *loss of privacy* if their work becomes too readily visible (Davidow & Malone, 1992). They may devote efforts to protecting their exchanges from outside influences, perhaps creating barriers to visibility or rejecting use of technology-mediated communication. Other teams may engage in extensive image management and attempt to influence how outsiders view the team, its processes, or its work products. There may be new threats to vigilant thinking due to more frequent interruptions and time and information overload. Since people can participate in more teams and more readily move in and out of teams, *cohesion and trust* within teams may be more difficult to maintain (Handy, 1995; Jarvenpaa & Leidner, in press). Ultimately, since people can belong to more teams yet act in unison with only a few, there may be the risk of team structures collapsing, leading to a dilution of "team" as a coherent, identifiable organizational structure. The study of virtual teams and their various approaches to managing interdependencies clearly presents a rich area for future research.

Implications at the Individual-Level

The virtual organization with its rich cauldron of interdependencies will bring significant opportunities and challenges to individuals within the corporation, both managers and non-managers alike. People will not nec-essarily resist this trend. Wageman (1995), for example found that people with high preferences for autonomy in their work grow accepting of interdependence over time and even come to prefer it. She found that the specific ways in which the structures and rewards of interdependent work relationships are designed shape individuals' preferences, their be-havior, how they experience rewards, and the impact of those rewards on their performance. Interdependence may also help to promote an individ-ual's identity within the collective such that he or she not only thinks of the "I" that operates in the firm but also the "we" who cumulatively form the larger enterprise (Agnew *et al.*, 1998; Brewer & Gardner, 1996; Weick & Roberts, 1993).

Viewed through the lens of interdependency, the challenge of the vir-tual organization for individuals is much more than simply managing information overload (Davidow & Malone, 1992; Hiltz & Turroff, 1985; Victor & Stephens, 1994). The more substantive difficulty lies in recogniz-ing, establishing, maintaining, and dissolving a continually changing set of interdependent relationships. Interdependency management involves identifying and anticipating one's interdependent relationships, seeking partners for relationships, selecting among potential partners, designing the structure of the interdependency, monitoring the exchange of infor-mation or other resources among the partners, deciding when and how to change the structure or other properties of the relationship, and reducing or eliminating unnecessary interdependencies as circumstances change. Supporting the virtual organization, therefore, requires more than a smooth sequence of workflows or a neatly engineered set of information systems. The need is for organizational design mechanisms that support a "complicated web of interdependencies" (Staudenmayer, 1997) that is continually formed and reformed.

Interdependency management may create a stimulating, energetic work environment, but if caretaking of interdependencies requires excessive managerial attention, the end result may be managerial symptoms such as role overload, role stress, or role conflict (Joyce, McGee & Slocum, 1997), regardless of whether organizational performance improves. To the extent that relationships are continually interrupted or in transition, individuals may experience a sense of time pressure, loss of control, or a decline in personal productivity. To cope effectively in virtual organizations, individuals most likely will have to pursue multiple, competing strategies to manage interdependencies, including: (1) efforts to *maintain* interdependencies, so that uncertainty can be reduced and operations made smooth; (2) efforts to *seek new interdependencies*, to enhance flexibility and opportunity for growth; and (3) efforts to *destroy existing interdependencies*, to streamline work and reduce coordination costs. Managers may or may not be explicitly aware of these mechanisms, even if they require substantial personal or organizational energy, if interdependency management becomes a part of everyday worklife in the virtual firm, and many interdependencies remain hidden and informal.

Interdependency management in virtual organizations clearly creates considerable challenges and opportunities for both practitioners and researchers. In the remainder of this Chapter, we highlight some of the exciting opportunities by exploring the use of a central management mechanism, information technology.

INFORMATION TECHNOLOGY AND THE MANAGEMENT OF INTERDEPENDENCIES

Information technology (IT), especially computer-based communication systems, has been offered as a critical mechanism for managing the virtual firm. Though there has been substantial research on the role of IT in support of new organizational forms (e.g., Beniger, 1990; Crowston & Malone, 1994; DeSanctis & Fulk, 1999; Henderson & Venkatraman, 1994; Lucas, 1996; Nohria & Berkeley, 1994), the precise ways in which IT can support formation, maintenance, and/or destruction of interdependencies remain unclear.

In recent thinking about virtual organizations, IT has been broadly conceived as a critical enabler of the virtual form, an essential capability that makes boundary-spanning across time, space and culture possible (Davidow & Malone, 1992; Holland, 1998). Without technology to link the nodes in the organizational network, the virtual organization could not exist. But IT can also be viewed as a tool for managerial control once virtual relationships are established. IT acts as an important integrating mechanism in the distributed organization, allowing otherwise disparate people and functions to link together (Karsten 1995, Malone, Yates & Benjamin 1987). In this way, IT can act as both input and outgrowth of new organizational forms (Fulk & DeSanctis, 1999). Finally, IT can be conceptualized as a context in which interdependencies occur as part of the organizational infrastructure in which interdependencies are designed, enacted, and redefined over time (Star & Ruhleder 1996). In fact, IT can take on multiple, overlapping roles in the virtual firm as follows:

Technology as Medium of Interdependency

At the most simplistic level, IT serves as a *conduit* between nodes in an interdependent relationship, a medium through which information or other resources can be exchanged between parties. In the multimedia environment of most modern firms, managers have choices about which type of medium to use within interdependent relationships, and different media may well have different impacts on efficiency, effectiveness, or the affective nature of relationships (Chidambaram & Jones, 1993; Daft & Lengel, 1986, Walther, 1992, 1995). Viewing technology as a medium through which interdependent relationships are connected suggests a contingency view of interdependencies. The goal is to select the right medium at the right time for the right task so that an efficient or effective exchange can take place among the parties. Using IT to support interdependency management is a matter of making appropriate media choices and arrangements.

Viewed purely as a medium of exchange, the trade-offs between face-to-face versus electronic communication can be compared (Daft, Lengel & Trevino, 1987), and alternative forms of electronic exchange can be evaluated for their effect on managerial performance and information flow (Dubrovsky, 1985; Trevino & Webster, 1992). For example, trust has been found to be difficult to form in electronic-based work settings (Jarvenpaa & Leidner, in press); status differential among parties can weaken in electronic communication (Dubrovsky, Kiesler & Sethna, 1991); and emotional exchange can be quite effective in electronic encounters (Walther, 1995). Such media effects have been shown to vary by contingencies such as the nature of the particular task at hand (Kraut *et al.*, 1992) and the pre-existing status differential among the parties (Weisband, Schneider & Connolly, 1995). As a result, decisions about how to link together the parties in an interdependent relationship are not trivial.

Technology as Trigger for Interdependency

Viewed as an instrument of organizational change, IT is a managerial mechanism for *creating* interdependent relationships. Here technology is more than a passive conduit and takes an active role in encouraging new interdependent relationships to form. These new interdependencies may be anticipated or unanticipated. Changes in the properties of an interdependency may occur as well. For example, providing e-mail to link various departments in the firm might lead to new collaborations, joint projects, or cross-functional teams that otherwise would not have formed. Similarly, consider a firm that installs an electronic discussion forum whereby customers can record suggestions for product improvement more easily and rapidly than through traditional mail or telephone media. At first glance, the technology provides a medium for managing the interdependency with customers. But the electronic forum also may lead to new interdependencies among the customers themselves, if, for example, the forum becomes a meeting place where customers talk with one another and identify common interests and possible ways to work together. What was designed as a medium to support a sequential flow of information from customer into, say, the product support group of a firm, may in fact lead to reciprocal exchanges among the customers themselves. From the perspective of the virtual organization, then, IT can support interdependency-seeking and transformation in the way in which work is managed.

Technology as Outcome or Result of Interdependency

Technology development, in the sense of new hardware, software, knowledge, or techniques, can occur as a *result* of interdependent relationships. Indeed, one of the hopes of relationships such as cross-functional teams is that innovation will result from lateral boundary spanning and blending of expertise across departments or functions. For instance, recent studies on knowledge management emphasizes the importance of maintaining and seeking ties for knowledge sharing and creation, so as to foster continuous knowledge generation and innovation (Hargadon, 1998; Nonaka & Konno, 1998). In this view, the real power of the virtual form is realized when relationships between otherwise unconnected entities produce some sort of new organizational product or process (Ring & Van de Ven, 1994).

Production of new technology can be deliberate, as in formal research and development collaborations, or unanticipated, as in emergent and unplanned initiatives. As an example of the latter, consider the current emphasis in many companies on building customized information systems to integrate various parts of the organization, such as customer orders and inventory management; SAP and PeopleSoft are current examples of these "enterprise-wide" systems (White, Clark & Ascarelli, 1997). Such systems are extensively refined and customized to meet the particular needs of interdependent relationships across functions, divisions, and/or geographical locations of a firm. The purpose is to develop IT systems to support the evolving interdependent work relationships that link the global enterprise. In other words, the need to connect interdependent employees drives the innovation of new technologies.

Technology as Context of Interdependency

Interdependent relationships occur in the social context of the larger enterprise, and technology infrastructure is increasingly viewed as part and parcel of that social context (Star & Ruhleder, 1996). Increasingly, IT is the *workspace* in which interdependencies are formed, maintained, and destroyed. As an example, consider how the creation of teams and their ongoing work takes place within LotusNotes environments or electronic learning spaces (Karsten 1995; Orlikowski *et al.*, 1995). Similarly, e-mail systems, electronic data exchange (EDE), intranets, extranets, and the like are forums in which enactment of interdependent relationships occur. Telephone, voice, and fax systems likewise provide contexts for exchange of information and movement of work inputs and outputs between individuals, groups, business units, and the firm at large.

Technology as context can be contrasted with the view of technology as medium. Whereas the view of technology as medium is physical, treating media as a conduit through which resources are exchanged, the contextual view is ecological. Technology is the petri dish or active culture in which many forms of interdependencies might grow. From this perspective, interdependent relationships in the virtual organization are so technology-infused that it makes no sense to consider a relationship without technology. Interdependencies either cannot occur, fail to thrive, or take on a distinctly different character without technology. Viewed as medium, technology is a conduit for linking entities that are interdependent, so the managerial choice is to decide which medium to use for a specific task. Viewed as context, technology is the rich background, or milieu, in which interdependencies are enacted. Managerial effort can be devoted to designing a desired technological context and fostering its growth, but the environment cannot be precisely engineered or fully specified.

These four perspectives, though not entirely distinct from one another, represent different approaches that researchers have taken to understanding the role of technology in organizations broadly. Each implies a somewhat different approach to the management of interdependencies in the virtual firm and spurs unique managerial and research questions. As a medium for resource exchange, the focal question to consider is: "How can we use technology to link with one another?" As a trigger for change the question becomes: "What new relationships can we form given the technology?" As a product of interdependent relationships, the key question is: "How might we produce new technologies as a result of interdependent relationships?" As a context for interdependency, the question becomes: "How should we operate (i.e., interrelate) in electronic workspaces? How can we communicate, design, negotiate, create, and so on?" Cumulatively, these perspectives point to a comprehensive understanding of how technology must be managed in support of interdependencies. All are vital to the advancement of the virtual enterprise.

CONCLUSION

Davidow and Malone (1992) suggested that two key aspects of organizations must be successfully managed in the virtual corporation: relationships and technology. Our analysis shows how interdependency can provide a powerful conceptual base for understanding these aspects of virtual forms. Through the lens of interdependency, the conundrum of the virtual organization becomes clear: interdependencies bring benefits, such as increased flexibility and shared resources, but they also imply costs, as interdependencies must be formed, nurtured and presumably destroyed and replaced with new relationships over time.

Identification and management of interdependencies are likely to be a key managerial challenge in the future, as increasing use of virtual forms at various levels of analysis results in a complex web of fluid and emergent interdependent relationships. At the same time, interdependencies present individuals, groups, and the organization at large with extensive choices regarding how interdependent work can be structured, formalized, extended beyond traditional corporate boundaries, made simple or complex, revealed or hidden, and so on. The opportunity to redefine interdependencies over time makes new organizational forms possible and presents occasions for using technology in multifaceted ways and enhancing innovation (Zajac, Golden & Shortell, 1991). These are the new challenges of organizational design, and they confront not only senior managers and strategists but individuals and small groups as well.

For organizational members, a key implication of our analysis is that active management of interdependencies and the use of technology for their support will be critical in the virtual setting. In the virtual organization, individuals are more responsible than in traditional organizations for seeking, maintaining, and destroying interdependent relationships. Increasingly, firms may need to develop systematic strategies for managing relationships both inside and outside corporate boundaries.

A key research thrust for the future will be: How can firms effectively manage the growth in interdependencies, the uneven pace of their development across the enterprise, and their changing properties? Critical areas for future research include the process of managing multiple relationships simultaneously—negotiating the conflicts of interest and time inherent in the complex web of virtual life. In addition, longitudinal studies of managing relationships over the entire course of their development, from creation through dissolution, will be needed. Cross-level studies that span individual, group, and organizational levels of analysis represent a third research opportunity. Finally, we urge further theorizing on and empirical analysis of the dynamics of interdependencies, especially those that are informal, hidden, or short-lived.

REFERENCES

Agnew, C. R., Rusbult, C. E., Van Lange, P. A. M. & Langston, C. A. (1998) Cognitive interdependence: commitment and the mental representation of close relationships. *Journal of Personality and Social Psychology*, **74**(4): 939–954.

Ancona, D. G. & Caldwell, D. F. (1987) Management issues facing new product teams in high technology companies. *Advances in Industrial and Labor Relations*, 199–221.

Barnard, C. (1948) *Organization and Management.* Cambridge, Mass: Harvard University Press.

Barner, R. (1996) The new millennium workplace: seven changes that will challenge managers and workers. *The Futurist*, **30**: 14–18.

Beniger, J.R. (1990) Conceptualizing information technology as organization, and *vice versa*. In J. Fulk & C. Steinfield (Eds), *Organizations and Communication Technology.* Newbury Park, CA: Sage.

Bleecker, S. E. (1994) The virtual organization. *The Futurist*, **March–April**, 9–14.

Brass, D. J. (1984) Being in the right place: a structural analysis of individual influence in an organization. *Administrative Science Quarterly*, **29**: 518–539.

Brewer, M. B. & Gardner, W. (1996) Who is this "we"? Levels of collective identity and self representations. *Journal of Personality and Social Psychology*, **1**(1): 83–93.

Burris, B. H. (1993) *Technocracy at work.* Albany, NY: State University of New York Press.

Chidambaram, L. & Jones, B. (1993) Impact of communication medium and computer support on group perceptions and performance: a comparison of face-to-face and dispersed meetings. *MIS Quarterly*, **17**(4): 465–492.

Clancy, T. (1994) The latest word from thoughtful executives—the virtual corporation, telecommuting and the concept of team. *Academy of Management Executive*, **8**(2): 8–10.

Coyle, J. & Schnarr, N. (1995) The soft-side challenges of the "virtual corporation". *Human Resource Planning*, **18**: 41–42.

Crowston, K. & Malone, T. W. (1994) Information technology and work organization. In T. J. Allen and M. S. Scott Morton (Eds), *Information Technology and the Corporation of the 1990s* (pp. 249–275), New York: Oxford University Press.

Daft, R. L. & Lengel, R. H. (1986) Organizational information requirements, media richness, and structural determinants. *Management Science*, 32: 554–571.

Daft, R. L., Lengel, R. H. & Trevino, L. K. (1987) Message equivocality, media selection, and manager performance: implications for information systems. *MIS Quarterly*, **11**: 355–366.

Davidow, W. H. & Malone, M. S. (1992) *The Virtual Corporation.* New York: Edward Burlingame Books/Harper Business.

DeSanctis, G. & Fulk, J. (Eds) (1999) *Shaping Organization Form: Communication, Connection, and Community* (pp. 473–495). Thousand Oaks, CA: Sage.

Dubrovsky, V. (1985) Real-time computer-mediated conferencing versus electronic mail. *Proceedings of the Human Factors Society,* 29th Annual Meeting, pp. 380–384.

Dubrovsky, V. J., Kiesler, S. & Sethna, B. N. (1991) The equalization phenomenon: status effects in computer-mediated and face-to-face decision-making groups. *Human–Computer Interaction,* 6: 119–146.

Dutton, W. H. (1999) The virtual organization: tele-access in business and industry. In G. DeSanctis & J. Fulk (Eds), *Shaping Organization Form: Communication, Connection, and Community.* Newbury Park, CA: Sage.

Ebers, M. (1997) *The Formation of Inter-organizational Networks.* Oxford: Oxford University press.

Eccles, R. G. & Crane, D. B. (1988) *Doing Deals: Investment Banks at Work.* Boston: Harvard Business School Press.

Eccles, R. G. & Nohria, N. (1992) On structure and structuring. In R. G. Eccles, N. Nohria & J. D. Berkley (Eds) *Beyond the Hype.* Boston, Harvard Business School Press.

Fulk, J. & DeSanctis, G. (1995) Electronic communication and changing organizational forms. *Organization Science,* 6(4): 1–13.

Galbraith, J. R. (1995) *Designing Organizations.* San Francisco, CA: Jossey-Bass.

Ghoshal, S. & Bartlett, C.A. (1990) The multinational corporation as an inter-organizational network. *Academy of Management Review,* **15**: 603–625.

Granovetter, M. (1985) Economic action and social structure: the problem of embeddedness. *American Journal of Sociology,* **91**(3): 481–510.

Gresov, C. (1990) Effects of dependence and tasks on unit design and efficiency. *Organization Studies,* **11**(4): 503–529.

Handy, C. (1995) Trust and virtual corporations. *Harvard Business Review,* **73**: 40–50.

Hargadon, A. B. (1998) Firms as knowledge brokers: lessons in pursuing continuous innovation. *California Management Review,* **40**(3): 209–228.

Hedberg, B., Dahlgren, G., Hansson, J. & Olve, N-G. (1997) *Virtual Organizations and Beyond: Discover Imaginary Systems.* New York: Wiley.

Henderson, J. C. & Venkatraman, N. (1994) Strategic alignment: a model for organizational transformation via information technology. In T. J. Allen & M. S. Scott Morton (Eds), *Information Technology and the Corporation of the 1990s* (pp. 202–220). New York: Oxford University Press.

Hiltz, S. R., & Turoff, M. (1985) Structuring computer-mediated communication systems to avoid information overload. *Communications of the ACM,* **28**(7): 680–689.

Holland, C. P. (1998) The importance of trust and business relationships in the formation of virtual organisations. In P. Sieber & J. Briese (Eds), *Organizational Virtualness: Proceedings of the VoNet Workshop* (April 27–28, pp. 53–64), Berne, Switzerland: Simowa Verlag.

Ibarra, H. (1992) Structural alignments, individual strategies, and managerial action: elements toward a network theory of getting things done. In N. Nohria and R.G. Eccles (Eds), *Networks and Organizations: Structure, Form, and Action* (pp. 165–188). Boston, Massachusetts: Harvard Business School.

Ibarra, H. & Andrews, S.B. (1993) Power, social influence, and sense making: effects of network centrality and proximity on employee perceptions. *Administrative Science Quarterly,* **38**: 277–303.

Jarillo, J. C. (1993) *Strategic Networks: Creating the Borderless Organization*. Oxford: Butterworth–Heinemann.

Jarvenpaa, S. L. & Leidner, D. (in press) Communication and trust in global virtual teams. *Organization Science*.

Jarvenpaa, S. L. & Shaw, T. R. (1998) Global virtual teams: Integrating models of trust. In P. Seiber & J. Griese (Eds), *Proceedings of the VoNet International Workshop on Organizational Virtualness*. University of Berne, Switzerland, April.

Joyce, W. F., McGee, V. E. & Slocum, J. W. (1997) Designing lateral organizations: an analysis of the benefits, costs, and enablers of nonhierarchical organizational forms. *Decision Sciences*, **28**(1): 1–25.

Karsten, H. (1995) Converging paths to Notes: in search of computer-based information systems in a networked company. *Information Technology & People*, 8(1): 7–34.

Kelley, H. H. & Thibaut, J. W. (1978) *Interpersonal Relations: A Theory of Interdependence*. New York: Wiley.

King, J. (1994) Network tools of the virtual corporation. *Network World*, **11**: 28–30.

Kraut, R., Galegher, J., Fish, R. & Chalfonte, B. (1992) Task requirements and media choice in collaborative writing. *Human–Computer Interaction*, 7: 375–407.

Kraut, R., Steinfield, C., Chan, A. P., Butler, B. & Hoag, A. (in press) Coordination and virtualization through electronic networks: empirical evidence from four industries. *Organization Science*.

Lawrence, P. R. & Lorsch, J. W. (1967) *Organization and Environment*. Cambridge, MA: Havard University Press.

Lipnack, J. & Stamps, J. (1997) *Virtual Teams: Reaching Across Space, Time and Organizations with Technology*. New York: Wiley.

Lockett, A.G. & Holland, C. P. (1996) The formation of a virtual global bank. *European Journal of IS*, **5**: 131–140.

Lucas, H. C., Jr. (1996) *The T-form Organization: Using Technology to Design Organizations for the 21st Century*. San Franciso: Jossey-Bass.

Malone, T. W., Yates, J. & Benjamin, R. I. (1987) Electronic markets and electronic hierarchies. *Communications of the ACM*, **30**: 484–496.

March, J. G. & Simon, H. A. (1958) *Organizations*. New York: McGraw-Hill.

Masciarelli, J. P. (1998) Are you managing your relationships? *Management Review*, **(April)**, 41–45.

McCann, J. & Ferry, D. L. (1979) An approach for assessing and managing interunit interdependence, *Academy of Management Review*, **4**: 113–119.

McDonald, T. (1995) Brain Trust: a new corporate climate favors loose, flexible, idea-based teams. *Successful Meetings*, **44**: 16.

McGrath, J. E. (1984) *Groups: Interaction and Performance*. Englewood Cliffs, NJ: Prentice-Hall.

Mitchell, T. R. & Silver, W. S. (1990) Individual and group goals when workers are interdependent: effects on task strategies and performance. *Journal of Applied Psychology*, **75**(2): 185–193.

Mowshowitz, A. (1994) Virtual organization: a vision of management in the information age. *The Information Society*, **10**: 267–288.

Nohria, N. & Berkley, J. D. (1994) The virtual organization: bureaucracy, technology, and the implosion of control. In C. Heckscher & A. Donnelon (Eds), *The Post-Bureaucratic Organization: New Perspectives on Organizational Change* (pp. 108–128), Thousand Oaks, CA: Sage.

Nonaka, I. & Konno, N. (1998) The concept of "Ba": building a foundation for knowledge creation. *California Management Review*, **40**(3): 40–45.

Orlikowski, W. J., Yates, J., Okamura, K. & Fujimoto, M. (1995) Shaping electronic communication: the metastructuring of technology in the context of use. *Organization Science*, **6**(4): 423–444,

Pfeffer, J. & Salacik, G. R. (1978) *The External Control of Organizations: A Resource Dependence Perspective*. New York: Harper and Row.

Powell, W. W. (1990) Neither market nor hierarchy: network forms of organization. In B. M. Staw & L. L. Cummings (Eds), *Research in Organizational Behavior*, (Vol. 12, pp. 295–336), Greenwich, Connecticut: JAI Press.

Ring, P. S. & Van de Ven, A. (1994) Developmental processes of cooperative interorganizational relationships. *Academy of Management Review*, **19**: 90–118.

Rusbult, C. E. (1983) A longitudinal test of the investment model: the development (and deterioration) of satisfaction and commitment in heterosexual involvements. *Journal of Personality and Social Psychology*, **45**(1): 101–117.

Rusbult, C. E., Johnson, D. J., *et al.* (1986) Predicting satisfaction and commitment in adult romantic involvements: an assessment of the generalizability of the investment model. *Social Psychology Quarterly*, **49**(1): 81–89.

Simons, T. (1995) Virtual reality. *Inc.*, **17**(14): 23–24.

Star, S. L. & Ruhleder, K. (1996) Steps toward an ecology of infrastructure: design and access for large information spaces. *Information Systems Research*, **7**(1): 111–134.

Staudenmayer, N. A. (1997) Managing multiple interdependencies in large scale software development projects, Unpublished Ph.D. Dissertation, The Sloan School of Management, Massachusetts Institute of Technology.

Thibaut, J. W. & Kelley, H. H. (1959) *The Social Psychology of Groups*. New York: Wiley.

Thompson, J. D. (1967) *Organizations in Action*. New York, McGraw Hill.

Tjosvold, D. (1986) The dynamics of interdependence in organizations. *Human Relations*, **39**(6): 517–540.

Trevino, L. K. & Webster, J. (1992) Flow in computer-mediated communication. *Communication Research*, **19**(5): 539–573.

Tushman, M. L. (1979) Work characteristics and subunit communication structure: a contingency analysis. *Administrative Science Quarterly*, **24**: 82–98.

Uzzi, B. (1997) Social structure and competition in interfirm networks: the paradox of embeddedness. *Administrative Science Quarterly*, **42**: 35–67.

Van de Ven, A., Delbecq, A. L. & Koenig, R. (1976) Determinants of coordination modes in organizations. *American Sociological Review*, **41**: 322–337.

Victor, B. & Blackburn, R. S. (1987) Interdependence: an alternative conceptualization. *Academy of Management Review*, **12**(3): 486–497.

Victor, B. & Stephens, C. (1994) The dark side of the new organizational forms: an editorial essay. *Organization Science*, **5**(4): 479–482.

Wageman, R. (1995) Interdependence and group effectiveness. *Administrative Science Quarterly*, **40**: 145–180.

Walther, J. B. (1992) Interpersonal effects in computer-mediated interaction: a relational perspective. *Communication Research*, **19**(1): 52–90.

Walther, J. B. (1995) Relational aspects of computer-mediated communication: experimental observations over time. *Organization Science*, **6**(2): 186–203.

Wegner, D. M. (1986) Transactive memory: a contemporary analysis of the group mind. In G. Mullen & G. Goethals (Eds), *Theories of Group Behavior*. New York: Springer-Verlag.

Wegner, D. M., Erber, R. & Raymond, P. (1991) Transactive memory in close relationships. *Journal of Personality and Social Psychology*, **61**(6): 923–929.

Wegner, D. M., Giuliano, T. & Hertel, P. T. (1985) *Cognitive Interdependence in Close Relationships. Compatible and Incompatible Relationships* (pp. 253–276). In W. J. Ickes. (Ed). New York: Springer-Verlag.

Weick, K. E. (1993)   Organizational redesign as improvisation. In G. P. Huber & W. H. Glick (Eds), *Organizational Change and Redesign* (pp. 346–379). New York: Oxford University Press.

Weick, K. E. & Roberts K. H. (1993)   Collective mind in organizations: heedful interrelating on flight decks. *Administrative Science Quarterly*, **38**: 357–381.

Weisband, S. P., Schneider, S. K. & Connolly, T. (1995)   Computer-mediated communication and social information: status salience and status differences. *Academy of Management Journal*, **38**(4): 1124–1151.

White, J., Clark, D. & Ascarelli, S. (1997)   Program of pain: this German software is complex, expensive—and wildly popular. *Wall Street Journal*, **March 14**, A1 and A12.

Zajac, E. J., Golden, B. R. & Shortell, S. M. (1991)   New organizational forms for enhancing innovation: the case of internal corporate joint ventures. *Management Science*, **37**(2): 170–184.

CHAPTER 7

Collaboration in the Virtual Organization

Susan G. Cohen and Don Mankin
University of Southern California, USA

INTRODUCTION

Collaboration is the key to effectiveness in the virtual organization. Faced with the growing challenges of global competition, rapid change, and increasing complexity, organizational structures are becoming more flexible and fluid (Mohrman, Galbraith & Lawler 1998). Advances in information technology have enabled people to work across organizational boundaries (Cohen & Mankin, 1998) and have provided the infrastructure for independent firms across the globe to function together as if they were a single company. The virtual corporate model depends upon people who can quickly come together and collaborate to exploit a specific opportunity or solve a specific problem. Virtual teams, composed of geographically dispersed organizational members who communicate and carry out their activities using technologies such as e-mail and videoconferencing depend upon effective collaborations for their success. Effective collaborations—among individuals, teams, and organizations–are the wellsprings of knowledge and creativity, key strategic resources for performance success in all modern organizations, but particularly in the virtual organization. Therefore, how to facilitate and support these collaborations should be the starting point for modern organizational and technological design. The purpose of this Chapter is to take this initial step and explore how organizations and technologies can be designed to create more effective collaborations.

Specifically, in this Chapter we examine four research traditions that provide some insight into the nature of the collaborative process and the factors that bear upon it. These areas are: (1) conflict-resolution; (2) pro-

Trends in Organizational Behavior, Volume 6. Edited by C. L. Cooper and D. M. Rousseau.
Copyright © 1999 John Wiley & Sons, Ltd.

cess facilitation and team design; (3) the psychology of flow and optimal experience; and (4) computer-supported cooperative work (CSCW). Three questions guide our exploration:

- What is the nature of collaboration?
- What processes, policies and structures enable collaboration?
- How can organizations create these enabling conditions that enable successful collaborations?

From this we construct a generic framework that integrates the under-standings that emerge from this exploration concerning: (1) the nature of the collaborative process; (2) the conditions and processes that can facilit-ate successful collaborations; and (3) the potential outcomes of this pro-cess. Then we briefly speculate on the implications of this framework for virtual teams and the virtual corporation.

CONFLICT RESOLUTION

The conflict resolution research views collaboration as a potential strate-gic intention or orientation of a person in a conflict situation. Thomas (1979, 1992) provides a two dimensional taxonomic scheme of the "strate-gic intentions" of the different parties involved in a conflict. Conflicting parties differ in their assertiveness, the degree to which each party at-tempts to satisfy his or her own concerns, and cooperativeness, the degree to which each party attempts to satisfy the other's concerns.

Five strategic intentions are classified in terms of these two orthogonal dimensions: competing, accommodating, compromising, avoiding, and collaborating. A *competing* intention represents an attempt to win one's position—to satisfy one's concern at the other's expense. This is a "win–lose" approach. An *accommodating* intention is an attempt to satisfy the other's concerns at the neglect of one's own. This is a "yielding–losing" approach where one helps the other achieve their goals at the expense of one's own goals or supports another opinion despite one's own reserva-tions. A *compromising* intention is understood as halfway between com-peting and accommodating. Compromising is an attempt to attain moderate but incomplete satisfaction of both parties' interests. Neither party is fully satisfied or fully dissatisfied. This approach can be viewed as "splitting the difference". An *avoiding* intention reflects a desire to ignore the concerns of both the self and the other. It involves withdraw-ing or exiting from the situation, not trying to shape it in any way.

Finally, a *collaborating* intention represents an attempt to fully satisfy the concerns of the two parties to achieve an integrated resolution.

Collaboration is a "win–win" approach where both parties' goals can be completely achieved. In judgmental conflicts, collaboration enables the parties to reach a synthesis—i.e., a new conclusion or idea that incorporates the insights of each party but goes beyond each. This taxonomy of five intentions is supported by relatively strong empirical evidence (Ruble & Thomas, 1976; Van de Vliert & Hordijk, 1989).

Roger Fisher and William Ury (1981) of the Harvard Negotiation Project in their book, *Getting to Yes*, describe an approach of *principled negotiation* based on collaboration. Their approach uses the following four-step process for coming to mutually acceptable agreements in every sort of conflict situation:

(1) Separate the people from the problem.
(2) Focus on interests, not positions.
(3) Invent options for mutual gain.
(4) Insist on using objective criteria.

The end result of principled negotiation is a "win–win" solution that satisfies both people's interests and provides the opportunity for mutual gain. The solution is new and often reflects a creative synthesis of ideas from both parties.

This research tradition helps us to understand collaboration. It reveals that collaboration can occur in conflictual and difficult situations. It is not necessary to begin with the same viewpoints to have a successful collaboration. In fact, a creative synthesis may occur precisely because the parties to the conflict begin with opposing viewpoints that are creatively integrated in the solution. Collaboration requires considerable communication skills—each party has to listen to the other's interest and voice their own—and be able to explore options that might meet both their interests. Resolving conflicts through principled negotiation creates shared understandings and new discoveries.

PROCESS FACILITATION AND TEAM DESIGN

Implicit in the definition of teams is a notion of collaboration. A team is a collection of individuals who are interdependent in their tasks, who share responsibility for outcomes, who see themselves and are seen by others as an intact social entity, embedded in one or more larger social system (for example, business unit or the corporation), and who manage their relationships across organizational boundaries (Cohen & Bailey, 1997; Hackman, 1987; and Alderfer, 1977). If tasks are interdependent and outcome responsibilities shared, then team members need to work with one another and relevant stakeholders to accomplish their goals. Working jointly with others is a necessary condition for collaboration, but as we will see shortly, not sufficient. Early and more recent work on team effectiveness from both a group process and a group design perspective addresses how members should work with one another.

For example, Benne and Sheats (1948) described the task functions and maintenance functions that should take place in groups in order for them to function effectively. Task functions include behaviors such as initiating, opinion seeking and giving, information seeking and giving, and summarizing. Maintenance functions included behaviors such as harmonizing and compromising, encouraging, diagnosing, and standard setting. According to Benne and Sheats (1948), these behaviors enable people to work together effectively in groups.

Edgar Schein's (1969) book, *Process Consultation*, extends Benne and Sheat's (1948) work and describes the characteristics of effective teams as shared goals, member participation and listening, free expression of ideas, mutual trust, effective problem-solving, consensus-seeking and testing, and flexibility and innovativeness. Many of these characteristics can be viewed as enablers of effective collaboration. If people who work with one another share goals, listen to one another, encourage participation, freely exchange ideas, trust one another, and so on, they are likely to work well together.

A more recent work from the same tradition is Roger Schwartz's (1994) book on facilitating effective groups. He lists 16 specific ground rules for effective groups such as: test assumptions and inferences, share relevant information, agree on what important words mean, disagree openly with any member of the group, discuss undiscussable issues, and do not take cheap shots or otherwise distract the group. Again, these ground rules can be viewed as the ingredients for a recipe on how to effectively collaborate with others.

The work on team design and effectiveness describes how to create the conditions for effective groups. The precursor of work in this tradition is the job characteristics model developed by Hackman and Oldham (1980). The primary focus of this model was on the design of individual jobs, but they extended the model to address the design of group tasks. Specifically, they argue that group members will experience high motivation in their work (and therefore, exert greater effort) when the following conditions are met:

(1) The group task requires the use of many different skills for successful completion (skill variety).
(2) The group task is a whole and meaningful piece of work (task identity).

(3) The outcomes of the group's work on the task "make a difference" to other people either inside or outside the organization (task significance).

(4) The group task provides substantial latitude for members to decide together how they will carry out the work, including the methods to be used, the assignment of priorities to various subtasks, the pace of the work, and so on (autonomy).

(5) The group as a whole receives trustworthy information, preferably from doing the work itself, about the adequacy of group performance (feedback). (pp. 171–172)

In his later chapter in the *Handbook of Organizations* (1987), Hackman develops this work further by presenting a model for team design and work group effectiveness. In this Chapter he asserts that group effectiveness is a function of the members' efforts, their knowledge and skills, and the appropriateness of their task performance strategies. The structure of the group and its task, the supportiveness of its organizational context, and the processes that the group uses create the conditions for effectiveness. The processes addressed by Hackman are coordination and commitment, sharing and weighing of expertise, and implementation of strategies. Similar to the work cited earlier, these process dimensions are likely to be enablers of collaboration. For example, how group members coordinate their efforts and their willingness to listen to one another and evaluate each others' contributions based on expertise (not on status or other task irrelevant characteristics) seem important for how well they collaborate together. Less obvious, but perhaps more critical, is the logic implied by this model for creating the conditions for effective collaboration. What can the organization do—in the way it structures groups and tasks, and in its systems, policies, and practices—to create the conditions for people to work together effectively. The focus on creating conditions for working together effectively enables us to look more comprehensively at the antecedents of collaboration.

In their recent review of the team effectiveness literature, Cohen and Bailey (1997) present a heuristic model that suggests that group effectiveness is a function of environmental factors, design factors, group processes, and group psychosocial traits. Environmental factors are characteristics of the external environment in which the organization is embedded, such as degree of turbulence. Design factors refer to those features of the group, task, and organization that can be directly manipulated to create the conditions for effective performance. Processes are interactions such as communication, decision-making and conflict resolution that take place within teams and with external others. Group psychosocial traits are shared understandings, beliefs, or emotional tone. This model extends the team design framework by drawing attention to the group as a social entity that has shared psychosocial traits that influence its behaviors. Group processes can become embedded in these traits, and these traits help to shape internal and external processes. The development of certain shared psychosocial traits may help to support collaboration. This framework helps us to look more comprehensively at the antecedents of and the conditions for effective collaboration.

THE PSYCHOLOGY OF FLOW AND OPTIMAL EXPERIENCE

The research tradition that offers great insight on the collaborative process does not even explicitly address this issue. Despite this limitation, the theories of "flow" and "optimal experience", as presented by the renowned cognitive psychologist, Mihaly Csikszentmihalyi (1990), provide a potentially rich phenomenological perspective from which to explore the process and experience of collaboration. He describes "optimal experience" as those "rare occasions" when "we feel a sense of exhilaration, a deep sense of enjoyment that is long cherished" (p. 3). In his theory, this experience is the result of "flow"—"the state in which people are so involved in an activity that nothing else seems to matter: the experience itself is so enjoyable that people will do it even at great cost, for the sheer sake of doing it" (p. 4).

According to Csikszentmihalyi there are eight major components to the flow experience. At least some have to exist for an activity to flow, to result in an optimal experience, and to be intensely enjoyed. Ultimately, it is these experiences that will produce the most effective, productive and, of special importance to him, creative results. These elements are:

- *A challenging activity that requires skill.* The activity is goal-directed and bounded by rules. The activity should be challenging but with a reasonable possibility of successful completion.
- *The merging of action and awareness.* The person's attention is completely absorbed by the activity and there is "no psychic energy left over to process any information but what the activity offers. All the attention is concentrated on the relevant stimuli. . . . People become so involved in what they are doing that the activity becomes spontaneous, almost automatic; they stop being aware of themselves as separate from the actions they are performing" (p. 53).
- *Clear goals and feedback.* Clear goals and immediate feedback are an important factor in achieving the level of involvement and focus described above.

- *Concentration on the task at hand.* When one is totally involved and focused on the task at hand . . . "one is able to forget all of the unpleasant aspects of life" (p. 58).
- *A sense of control.* What people enjoy, Csikszentmihalyi argues, "is not the sense of being in control, but the sense of exercising control in difficult situations. It is not possible to experience a feeling of control unless one is willing to give up the safety of protective routines. Only when a doubtful outcome is at stake, and a person is able to influence that outcome, can a person really know whether she is in control" (p. 61).
- *The loss of self-consciousness.* "The loss of the sense of self separate from the world around it is sometimes accompanied by a feeling of union with the environment" (p. 63). The apparent paradox is that the loss of self during the flow experience is often followed by the emergence of a stronger sense of self after the experience ends. Csikszentmihalyi describes it as follows:

> "In flow a person is challenged to do her best, and must constantly improve her skills. At the time, she doesn't have the opportunity to reflect on what this means in terms of the self—if she did allow herself to become self-conscious, the experience could not have been very deep. But afterward when the activity is over and self-consciousness has a chance to resume, the self that the person reflects upon is not the same self that existed before the flow experience: it is now enriched by new skills and fresh achievements." (pp. 65–66)

Csikszentmihalyi does not specifically address the collaborative process but he does apply his theory to work tasks and to interpersonal relationships within families and among friends. In any case it is not difficult to see how his theory and the elements described above could be used to help us understand the collaborative process. Following his principles we can see that successful collaborative experiences are very enjoyable and productive. They work best when the activities are directed toward clear goals, the collaborators possess the skills required by the task, and the goals are challenging but reasonably attainable. Anybody who has been part of a successful collaboration also knows the importance of immediate feedback from teammates and co-workers in sustaining the collaborative relationship and progress toward their mutual goals. They also will recognize the focus, the total absorption and timelessness, the sense of control and the immersion of the self in the totality of the collaborative moment that Csikszentmihalyi describes. Most important, anybody who has ever been in an effective collaborative relationship has experienced the sheer pleasure Csikszentmihalyi talks about in other contexts when collaborations work well, or to use his expression, when they "flow".

COMPUTER-SUPPORTED COOPERATIVE WORK (CSCW)

The research tradition on computer-supported cooperative work explicitly focuses on collaborative intellectual work. As defined by Galegher and Kraut (1990) the aims of researchers in this field are:

> "... to describe both the general features of collaborative intellectual work and the specific details of particular kinds of collaboration, to create technological systems that will improve the quality and efficiency of collaborative work and foster kinds of collaboration that would be impossible without advanced communication and computer support, and to assess the impact of these technologies on individuals, groups, and organizations." (p. 4)

Not surprisingly, the focus of most of the work in this area is on the technology for facilitating collaboration, commonly known as groupware, not on the nature of the collaborative process itself.

Nonetheless, some interesting ideas can be found in the literature, especially in the book by Michael Schrage, appropriately titled, *Shared Minds: The New Technologies of Collaboration* (1990). In contrast with many writers in this area, Schrage spends a considerable amount of time discussing the nature of collaboration before moving on to the primary topic of his book, the technology of collaboration. He begins by differentiating between "communication", which by inference is the primary focus of much of the CSCW literature, and "collaboration". Communication, he notes, is merely the exchange or transmission of information, collaboration is the act of constructing relevant meanings that can be shared by all parties to the collaboration. "The act of collaboration is an act of shared creation and/or shared discovery" (p. 6) in which "two or more individuals with complementary skills [interact] to create a shared understanding that none had previously possessed or could have come to on their own" (p. 40).

> "Organizations that attempt to substitute increased communication for increased collaboration will learn the hard way that there is a tremendous difference. Flooding someone with more information doesn't necessarily make him a better thinker. Creating a shared understanding is simply a different task than exchanging information. It's the difference between being deeply involved in a conversation and lecturing to a group. The words are different, the tone is different, the attitude is different, and the tools are different." (p. 7)

Effective communication is only a precursor, a necessary but not a sufficient condition for collaboration.

According to Schrage, shared "space" is essential for effective collaboration so that individual collaborators can "play collectively with ideas and information" and "generate shared understandings that they couldn't possibly have achieved on their own" (pp. 31–32). He describes other characteristics associated with successful collaboration. It is "purposive" (i.e., the purpose is to solve a problem or create or discover something) and occurs within constraints, including limits of expertise, time, money, the competition, and the "prejudices of the day".

THE RINGS OF COLLABORATION: A FRAMEWORK OF OUTCOMES, ENABLERS AND THE PROCESS ITSELF

Figure 7.1 summarizes much of the proceeding discussion by integrating many of the elements, definitions, and conditions that emerge from the four research traditions. Each concentric ring represents the factors and processes that directly impact the factors and processes in the next inner concentric ring, and the outcomes represented by the innermost ring. The factors and processes in the outer rings directly impact those in the inner rings by creating conditions and by setting constraints. This framework intentionally does not show specific causal relationships. We believe that causality can be multiply determined, reciprocal, and dynamic. For example, the competitive environment in which a firm is embedded influences the organizing policies and culture, and may also have direct influences on task design. In addition, the structures that are close antecedents may shape collaborative processes, but the use of collaborative processes may shape the structures that develop. If people have succeeded in producing creative outcomes through past collaborations, then they may be more likely to engage in new endeavors and use the processes that led to their past success.

The innermost ring presents the ultimate focus of the inquiry, the reason why we are even interested in the collaborative process—i.e., successful, productive and value-added outcomes. These outcomes are creative—new understandings and insights, new products and services, improved processes, solutions to problems, etc.—not just producing the same goods over and over, or providing routine, ongoing services. The discussion in the last several pages suggests that creativity is the direct result of the collaborative process itself. An associated outcome is the feeling of satisfaction, the exhilaration and enjoyment that accompanies the successful achievement of a challenging goal.

We use Schrage's definition as the starting point for understanding the fundamental nature of the collaborative process, the next innermost ring. The act of collaboration involves "two or more individuals with complementary skills interacting to create a shared understanding that none had previously possessed or could have come to on their own" (p. 40). When

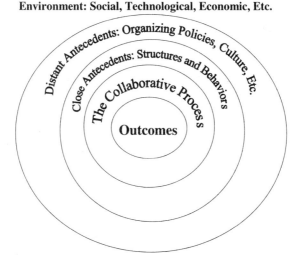

Figure 7.1   Rings of collaboration

it works well, collaborators build upon each others ideas, going back and forth, constructing an upward spiral of new, shared ideas until the process concludes with the creative outcomes in the innermost ring. New ideas arise from the synthesis of individual ideas, a creative synergy emerging from the building blocks of the collaborative process.

This process is not always as smooth as this description might imply. The *sine qua non* of effective collaboration is the tension and conflict between different ideas, viewpoints, and objectives. As we have seen from the conflict–resolution literature, conflict when managed well can spark creativity; on the other hand, it can destroy the collaboration when it is suppressed, mishandled, or allowed to escalate unchecked. This may seem to contradict our earlier point that participants will experience exhilaration and enjoyment as the outcome of a successful collaboration. But that is the case only if we "take the temperature" of the process at various points as it unfolds rather than look at the entire process from the perspective of its ultimate outcome. Most people who have been parties to successful collaborations would probably describe them as often difficult, sometimes painful, but ultimately profoundly satisfying in a way that only the successful conclusion of a difficult journey can be.

They might also describe the process as thoroughly involving, transcendent, and timeless, especially when the collaborators have managed to resolve critical conflicts and are well on their way to constructing the upward spiral of creative synthesis, brick by brick, idea by idea. The focus, concentration, loss of self consciousness, and merging of action and awareness described by Csikszentmihalyi is also part of the collaborative experience.

The next ring of the framework describes what we refer to as the "close antecedents" of the process. That is, they are the immediate enablers of collaboration, the conditions that most directly impact the collaborative process. We partition these conditions into two categories: structures and behaviors. In the first category we include characteristics of the tasks and the conditions that make up the immediate environment within which the tasks are performed. The job design and group design literature suggests that the most important may be task interdependence—i.e., the degree to which the successful completion of tasks by one individual is dependent upon the successful completion of other tasks by other individuals. If tasks are not interdependent there is no need or reason to collaborate. Individuals working alone can do the work. Attempts to create collaboration and teamwork in this case will be forced, artificial, and ultimately, ineffective.

Another important set of close antecedents are the group task characteristics described earlier on in the section on team design, especially the five characteristics associated with highly motivating group tasks identified by Hackman and Oldham—skill variety, task identity, task significance, autonomy, and feedback (see Hackman & Oldham, 1980; p. 6). Other structural characteristics that emerge from the review earlier in this Chapter include clear and challenging goals, as well as constraints and rules that place some limits on the collaborative process. It may seem illogical to classify rules and constraints as enablers, but without boundaries and structure placed on the process, collaborators can easily lose focus and be overwhelmed by the choices offered by limitless options. Another characteristic is the task-related skills and expertise of the participants. They are obviously critical factors in successful collaborations.

The last structural characteristic is shared space. This notion is central to Schrage's perspective on collaboration. He argues that the primary obstacle to effective collaboration is the "ephemeral" nature of conversation.

> "Even under the best of circumstances, its difficult to keep track of what's been said in conversation . . . the words vanish the instant they've been uttered. Even when taking notes, one can rarely, if ever, get a perfect transcript because of the inevitable discrepancies between what's been said and what's heard. . . . Conversations don't have memories, only their participants do. The serial and ephemeral nature of conversation, then subtly works against collaboration." (Schrage, 1990; pp. 97–98)

Therefore, collaboration requires a means for capturing the ideas discussed by participants and displaying them so that all can see, examine, analyze, manipulate, synthesize and build upon them to create shared understandings and new ideas. Whether it be a sodden bar napkin covered with notes and equations, a blackboard, or a computer-driven projection screen, there needs to be a "space"—physical or electronic—where the ideas and symbols are displayed and "shared" so that everyone can participate on an equal footing.

The second category of close antecedents is the cognitive and interpersonal behaviors, skills and processes that ultimately make collaborations possible. The behaviors described earlier in the section on process consultation can all be direct enablers of the collaborative process. It is easy to see how behaviors and norms concerning participation, listening, free expression of ideas, and trust can contribute to effective collaborations. In addition, the sixteen "ground rules" for effective groups offered by Roger Schwartz provide very specific recommendations that can help create successful collaborations.

Other writers have also talked about the importance of "lateral skills" in cross-functional collaborations. Mankin, Cohen and Bikson (1996) define lateral skills, as the ability to work with and learn from other individuals with different functional backgrounds, perspectives, and agendas. People with lateral skills can:

- act as a bridge and interpreter between collaborators from different functional areas,
- can recognize the relevance of others' expertise and rapidly learn their professional language and concepts, and
- can acknowledge the validity of others' points of view even when they differ from their own.

It is easy to see how lateral skills can facilitate collaboration, especially among participants with diverse backgrounds, perspectives, and agendas.

The outermost ring of the framework contains the more distant antecedents of collaboration, the organizational policies, programs, structures, systems and culture that support collaboration. Included here are compensation systems that reward collaboration and teamwork, and training and education to help individuals learn the interpersonal process skills described above. Also important are professional development programs that encourage lateral career moves and networking. In fact, anything that helps lower boundaries and generally makes it easier for people to work together is necessary for organizations committed to innovation and knowledge-based change. New technologies, policies or cultures will play critical roles in reducing barriers to collaboration, whether they be organizational, functional, hierarchical, temporal, geographical or attitudinal in nature (see Mankin, Cohen & Bikson, 1996).

And to complete our framework, all of these rings, all of these conditions, processes and outcomes are embedded within an environment that is increasingly competitive, dynamic, unpredictable and global in scope.

Changes in societies, economies, technologies, ideas, values and knowledge are the context for collaboration, as well as the drivers that will make it so critical for success in the 21st century.

IMPLICATIONS FOR VIRTUAL ORGANIZATIONS AND TEAMS

We began this Chapter by asserting that collaboration is the key to effectiveness in the virtual organization. We then presented a framework that integrated the understandings about collaboration that emerge from four research traditions—conflict resolution, process facilitation and team design, the psychology of flow and optimal experience, and computer supported cooperative work. This framework describes the collaborative process itself, the factors that create the conditions for collaboration to occur, and finally, the outcomes that are expected to emerge. In this final section, we look more closely at the virtual organization and virtual teams, and discuss the implications of "virtuality" for collaboration.

Virtual organizations are more complex than traditional organizations, in that they connect multiple organizations in a dynamic network. Each organization has its own policies, systems, and structures that may not easily mesh with its partners. The dynamic nature of the network, as well as the number of boundaries that are crossed, increase uncertainty and complexity. Similarly, virtual teams connect people across disciplines, functions, geographies, and organizations to temporarily work together on particular opportunities. In contrast to a traditional work team, whose members report to the same supervisor in the same unit of the same organization, virtual team members report to different supervisors from different functions, disciplines, and potentially different organizations, and do not share common methods of working together. Virtual team members need to develop their own methods of working together. In order to deal with the uncertainty and complexity, and to successfully develop effective ways of working together, collaboration is essential.

Collaboration enables people who cut across multiple boundaries to develop a common focus. Virtuality results in fragmentation without sustained effort to develop this common focus. Members of virtual teams cannot depend upon following the same policies and operating procedures, belonging to the same culture, using the same systems, and reporting to their boss in the same organizational structure in order to keep them focused in a common direction. Instead, a shared understanding emerges from the processes of collaboration. The rules for working together are not embedded in the operating procedures or shared cultural norms of a given organization. Things that normally would be taken for granted are not in place.

Consequently, the difficulty of developing this shared understanding for those connected virtually should not be underestimated. Virtual teams need to create new structures that enable them to stay focused and create shared understandings about how they will work together and the results they are trying to achieve. This calls for putting in place many of the same conditions and processes that enable traditional teams to work effectively, but being more intentional and explicit about doing this. For example, having an interdependent task, and defining shared goals and making sure that all members have a common understanding of them are critical. Developing common working procedures and processes is essential. Ensuring that resources are allocated for the work at hand is a responsibility of virtual teams and members may need to negotiate for resources with their home organization. Creating "shared space" where the work of the team is represented so that all can see, becomes even more important when people are not co-located. The explicit use of systematic decision-making processes, a success factor for all teams (Mohrman, Cohen & Mohrman, 1995), may be even more important for virtual teams. Explicitly deciding to use good group processes helps a virtual team develop common and productive ways of working together. The processes and behaviors that we describe as the close antecedents of collaboration are particularly important for virtual teams and people networked in virtual organizations.

Organizations that use virtual teams and the organizations that are linked together to form virtual organizations should examine their policies, systems, structures, and culture to see if they support collaboration. As discussed earlier, reward systems that support teamwork and professional development systems that encourage lateral movement and networking help to reduce barriers to collaboration, both within and across organizations. The information technology systems that are used deserve special comment, because they enable people to communicate across geographic and organizational boundaries. The information technology designs that are used should enable users of one system to communicate and work with users of other systems—directly, seamlessly, and transparently. That means that systems need to be compatible with one another, preferably using open, non-proprietary standards (Mankin, Cohen & Bikson, 1996). Information technology also enables collaborative work to be archived, stored, reviewed and modified by all team members, irrespective of location. Information technology provides the platform for collaboration in the virtual organization—by linking people together and creating an electronic "shared space" where ideas can be synthesized and discoveries captured.

Information technology provides the platform, but ultimately it is the people that make collaboration work. The importance of the human element and human connections should not be taken for granted, particularly where people are connected virtually. At some fundamental level, it comes down to trust. Managers need to trust their people to give them the freedom to work virtually—where they cannot be seen and accounted for moment by moment. People need to trust others from different backgrounds, disciplines, organizations, and countries in order to effectively collaborate with them. Without trust, according to Charles Handy, the virtual organization cannot work at all:

> "If it is even true that a lack of trust makes employees untrustworthy, it does not bode well for the future of virtuality in organizations. If we are to enjoy the efficiencies and other benefits of the virtual organization, we will have to rediscover how to run organizations based more on trust than on control. Virtuality requires trust to make it work: technology on its own is not enough." (Handy, 1995; p. 44)

In its essence, collaboration involves personal relationships between people. People need to relate to one another in order to build upon each other's ideas and create something new. It involves the willingness to trust someone enough to work through a conflict with them and to transcend the difficulties that differences always pose. This is true for all organizations, but becomes a special challenge in the virtual organization that cannot rely on informal contact to build these relationships. By explicitly creating processes and systems that support collaboration, virtual teams and organizations create the conditions for these personal relationships to develop. For the organizations and people that are willing to invest in creating the conditions and relationships for collaboration—the new discoveries, creative insights, and the exhilaration and satisfaction that results from achieving challenging goals—are well worth the investment.

REFERENCES

Alderfer, C. P. (1977) Group and intergroup relations. In J. R. Hackman & J. L. Suttle (Eds), *Improving the Quality of Work Life* (pp. 227–296). Palisades, C.A.: Goodyear.

Benne, K. & Sheats, P. (1948) Functional roles of group members. *Journal of Social Issues*, **2**: 42–47.

Cohen, S. G. & Bailey, D. E. (1997) What makes teams work: group effectiveness research from the shop floor to the executive suite. *Journal of Management*, **23**(3): 239–290.

Cohen, S. G. & Mankin, D. (1998) The changing nature of work: managing the impact of information technology. In S. A. Mohrman, J. R. Galbraith, E. E. Lawler, III *et al.* (Eds), *Tomorrow's Organization: Crafting Winning Capabilities in a Dynamic World* (pp. 154–178). San Francisco: Jossey Bass.

Csikszentmihalyi, M. (1990) *Flow: The Psychology of Optimal Experience.* New York: Harper & Row.

Fisher, R. & Ury, W. (1981)   *Getting to Yes: Negotiating Agreement Without Giving In.* New York: Penguin Books.

Galegher, J. and Kraut, R. E. (1990)   Technology for intellectual work: perspectives on research and design. In Galegher, J., Kraut, R. E. & Egido, C. (Eds), *Intellectual Teamwork: Social and Technological Foundations of Cooperative Work* (pp. 1–20). Hillsdale, NJ: Erlbaum.

Hackman, J. R. (1987)   The design of work teams. In J. W. Lorsch (Ed.), *Handbook of Organizational Behavior* (pp. 315–342). Englewood Cliffs, NJ: Prentice-Hall.

Hackman, J. R. & Oldham, G. R. (1980). *Work Redesign.* Reading, MA: Addison-Wesley.

Handy, C. (1995)   Trust and the virtual organization. *Harvard Business Review,* **73**(3): 40–50.

Mankin, D., Cohen, S. C. & Bikson, T. K. (1996)   *Teams and Technology: Fulfilling the Promise of the New Organization.* Boston: Harvard Business School Press.

Mohrman, S. A., Cohen, S. G. & Morhman, A. M. (1995)   *Designing Team-based Organizations: New Forms for Knowledge Work.* San Francisco: Jossey Bass.

Mohrman, S. A., Galbraith, J. R., Lawler, E. E., III, & Associates (1998)   *Tomorrow's Organization: Crafting Winning Capabilities in a Dynamic World.* San Francisco: Jossey Bass.

Ruble, T. L. & Thomas, K. W. (1976)   Support for a two-dimensional model of conflict behavior. *Organizational Behavior and Human Performance,* **16**: 143–155.

Schrage, M. (1990)   *Shared Minds: The New Technologies of Collaboration.* New York: Random House.

Schein, E. (1969)   *Process Consultation: Its Role in Organization Development.* Reading, Mass: Addison-Wesley.

Schwartz, R. (1994)   *The Skilled Facilitator: Practical Wisdom for Developing Effective Groups.* San Francisco: Jossey Bass.

Thomas, K. W. (1979)   Conflict. In S. Kerr (Ed.), *Organizational Behavior* (pp. 151–181). Columbus, Ohio: Grid Publications.

Thomas, K. W. (1992)   Conflict and negotiation process in organizations. In M. D. Dunnette & L. M. Hough (Eds), *Handbook of Industrial and Organizational Psychology, 2nd Edition (Vol. 3,* pp. 655–717). Palo Alto, California: Consulting Psychologists Press, Inc.

Van de Vliert, E. & Hordijk, J. W. (1989). A theoretical position of compromising among other styles of conflict management. *Journal of Social Psychology,* **129**: 681–690.

Index